napa bulletin 20

Careers in Anthropology
Profiles of Practitioner
Anthropologists

■ Paula L. W. Sabloff, ed.

National Association for the Practice of Anthropology
A section of the American Anthropological Association

NAPA Bulletins are occasional publications of the National Association for the Practice of Anthropology, a section of the American Anthropological Association.

Linda Bennett and Dennis Wiedman
General Editors

Library of Congress Cataloging-in-Publication Data

Careers in anthropology: profiles of practitioner anthropologists / Paula L. W. Sabloff, ed.
  p.   cm.—(NAPA bulletin; 20)
  ISBN 0-913167-98-3
  1. Anthropology—Vocational guidance. I. Sabloff, Paula L. W. II. National Association for the Practice of Anthropology (U.S.). III. Series.

GN41.8 .C37 2000
301'.023—dc 21
  00-042049

ISBN 0-913167-98-3

www.NAPABulletin.org

Contents

Introduction

Paula L. W. Sabloff
University of Pennsylvania Museum of Archaeology and Anthropology
and Department of Anthropology

This book has grown out of a series of practitioner profiles that Susan Squires and I published in the *Anthropology Newsletter* of the American Anthropological Association from 1994 to 1997. Building on the brief descriptions of practitioner career profiles organized by Karin Tice, the secretary/editor of NAPA, we networked with our NAPA colleagues and friends. We asked them to write about their career paths—from undergraduate and graduate school training to obtaining employment—and to describe their current jobs. We suggested that authors include their philosophies about their career paths and any suggestions they might have for young people contemplating or preparing for careers as practitioner anthropologists. The reader will see that different authors have emphasized different points.

All authors were incredibly sincere and concerned about helping young people plan career paths. Many thanked us for the opportunity to reflect on their work lives, to stop and think about anthropology, and to recommit themselves to linking their anthropological ideals with their work.

This bulletin is an expansion and update of many profiles published in the *Anthropology Newsletter*. All authors were given the opportunity to revise their practitioner profiles, and most have done so. The dates of original publication and updated material are provided so that the reader can place each profile in historical context. Also, for additional profiles, I networked with archaeologists and anthropological linguists to ensure that the book covers all four fields of anthropology—sociocultural, biological, archaeological, and linguistic anthropology. In this way, the book would reflect the field and complement the NAPA–produced video, *Anthropologists at Work,* a presentation of anthropologists' work in applied and practicing anthropology.

I was successful in finding archaeologists to contribute to this volume. I had difficulty locating anthropological linguists. Perhaps this was because my network does not extend far into this particular anthropological community. At any rate, the lack of representation of anthropological linguists in this book is a deficit I wish I could have overcome.

The reader will notice that the practitioners in the book seem to draw on two basic definitions of culture. Some who refer to the holistic, or systemic, approach to anthropology are working from the original perspective of culture propounded by E. B. Tylor, who wrote, "Culture or Civilization, taken in its wide ethnographic sense, is that complex whole which includes knowledge, belief, art, morals, law, custom, and any other capabilities and habits acquired by man as a member of society" (1871:1). This definition set the agenda for anthropological work for 100 years. Based on the idea that a society can be isolated from its physical and historical context, Tylor's definition does the following:

- It conceptualizes culture as a core of beliefs, attitudes, and values shared by a group of people, a society. It is these shared perceptions (or worldview) that make the population homogeneous and set it apart from surrounding groups (see Wright 1998:8).
- And it notes that the major characteristic of any culture is that it is holistic. This means two things: First, culture—the worldview of a society—affects all parts of group thinking and acting. That is, culture penetrates daily life in all its manifestations. Second, culture is holistic because all parts of a culture are interrelated. Another way of saying this is that a culture is a system with interdependent parts. If, for example, the political structure changes—through invasion, colonialism, natural disaster, and so on—then we can expect the economic and religious parts of the society to change; we can expect the socialization and enculturation processes to also change.

This kernel of Tylor's definition—that culture has a cognitive base and is systemic—has informed anthropological research and has contributed to the understanding of culture in many disciplines. It is our strength and part of our contribution to social science. Tylor's definition is still in use today and is the foundation for the work of many of the practitioners profiled in this volume.

In 1973 a new definition of culture coalesced in the writing of Clifford Geertz. He writes, "Believing, with Max Weber, that man is an animal suspended in webs of significance he himself has spun, I take culture to be those webs, and the analysis of it to be therefore not an experimental science in search of law but an interpretive one in search of meaning" (1973:5). His spider imagery may be interpreted as follows:

- Culture is the meaning that groups of people give to things they observe or experience. For example, some people understand lightening as a sign that God (or the gods) is angry, whereas others interpret it as an electric current resulting from friction between clouds.
- The meaning that people give to things is encoded in symbols, for example, the flag, certain foods, body language. Every culture has "key symbols"—symbols that are reminders of how people should behave and how people should view "reality." The combination of symbols is sometimes called a people's ideology (Wright 1998:9).

- A culture is not coterminous with a territory or group. One person can keep several cultures in her or his head at any one time and switch back and forth between them as the situation demands. Several cultures can occupy the same space (for example, over 146 languages are spoken in New York City). And one culture can be spread over vast noncontiguous spaces (for example, Mongolian culture is practiced in the People's Republic of Mongolia, Inner Mongolia, Germany, and the United States where there are enclaves of Mongolians).
- Culture is a process. At any one time, there are several perspectives in a culture. Men and women contribute different meaning to a given event; so do ethnic groups (Americans' reactions to the O. J. Simpson trial provide a good example of this). These different meanings are "contested meanings" because groups compete in the public arena to have their meanings/ideology predominate (see Wright 1998). Thus, culture becomes a constant process of "contestation."

This new definition of culture enables us to apply an old concept to the modern world of complex societies and to all societies facing globalization. Geertz's definition underpins several practitioner profiles in the book.

No matter which definition the practitioners subscribe to, I hope the reader will see that the concept of culture binds together all four fields of anthropology in academic, applied, and practitioner work. I hope the reader will also see the idealism in the practitioners' lives. These authors recognize that anthropology has made major contributions to society and social science, for it is the discipline that has spawned the concepts of culture, cultural relativism, and cultural preservation and—most important for practitioner and applied work—the idea that the best way to solve human problems and understand the issues is to include the perspective of the people being affected by change, that is, the bottom-up approach to social change.

I would like to thank the NAPA Board for suggesting this bulletin. It is gratifying to know that my previous work is considered valuable, especially for the people I care about most: students and future colleagues. My NAPA colleagues are the ones I know best—friendly, inclusive, supportive, intellectually stimulating, can-do people. My association with them is always a pleasure. My thanks go especially to Linda Bennett and Dennis Wiedman, coeditors of the NAPA Bulletin Series. They have supported and encouraged this project (and me) from its inception. Linda was especially helpful in pushing this manuscript through to completion, and she deserves the credit for the highly effective idea of placing major ideas in bold throughout the text. Megan Tracy, a Ph.D. candidate in anthropology at the University of Pennsylvania, made the project possible through her careful administrative and editing efforts. And my husband, Jeremy A. Sabloff, makes everything possible through his love and support.

References Cited

Geertz, Clifford
    1973   The Interpretation of Cultures. New York: Basic Books.
Tylor, E. B.
    1871   Primitive Culture: Researches into the Development of Mythology, Philosophy, Religion, Language, Art, and Custom, vol. 1. London: J. Murray.
Wright, Susan
    1998   The Politicization of "Culture." Anthropology Today 14(1):7–15.

April 1998
Revised, summer 1999
Ulaanbaatar and Philadelphia

Putting Anthropology to Work

Darby Stapp
Battelle Memorial Institute

Darby Stapp, Umatilla Indian Reservation, 1996

During my freshman year in college, I took an Anthropology 100 course quite by accident and immediately realized that anthropology was the field for me. I soon switched my major and embarked on a journey that would take me to remote regions of the western United States; Gujarat, India; and ultimately to the center of the largest environmental cleanup program in the world. This is the U.S. Department of Energy's (DOE) Hanford Site, in southeastern Washington State.

I work as a senior development engineer at Pacific Northwest National Laboratory, one of the DOE multiprogram laboratories. The laboratory is operated by **Battelle Memorial Institute, a not-for-profit research and development organization dedicated to putting technology to work for the betterment of humankind.** My work is focused on projects that seek to (1) prevent environmental degradation by eliminating or minimizing the generation of waste and (2) restore the environment by cleaning up sites contaminated with chemical and radioactive materials. Over the last few years, I have managed or participated in projects such as assessing performance of a major cleanup program at Hanford, developing public involvement programs for cleanup projects in Alaska, identifying technology needs for the nation's low-level radioactive waste program, assessing the global environmental impact of solid waste, developing methods for incorporating stakeholder values in cleanup decisions at Hanford, and designing a co-management (DOE and Indian tribes) cultural resource program at Hanford.

Recently, a new door has opened for me at Hanford. **I have left Battelle and joined an environmental remediation firm** (CH2M Hill Hanford, Inc.) primarily to address Native American concerns related to the cleanup of the Hanford Site, a 50-year, $60 billion endeavor. **We will be striving to implement a collaborative cultural resource management program at Hanford with the Native American tribes that claim Hanford as their ancestral lands.** It will be good to return to a job that relates more directly to my specific anthropological skills, but I remain as convinced as ever that the future of anthropology lies outside the current academic boundaries of the discipline.

How did an anthropologist get involved in work such as this? My career began in the late 1970s at the University of Denver studying prehistoric North American cultures. I took my first applied anthropology course my senior year, a course that opened my eyes to the vast opportunities for anthropology in the real world. At the University of Idaho, where I earned my M.A., I concentrated on historic Native American culture in the Pacific Northwest and began working in cultural resource management projects. I then moved to the University of Pennsylvania to study for my Ph.D.; there I concentrated on American culture and wrote a dissertation focused on a multiethnic mining community of Idaho.

In 1987, I received an **offer to join Battelle as a communications specialist. Here was a chance to join the world of the future and explore ways that anthropology could contribute to humanity, and the decision to leave the university was an easy one.** At Battelle, I worked with a variety of researchers, helping them translate their complex technical research into something people could understand. The communication skills I learned and the insights I gained about the relationship between technology and culture have proven invaluable. After a few years, the urge to get back to making technical contributions led me to move within the company to an environmental cleanup department, where I began managing projects and contributing in areas in which human issues came into play. Being selected by the U.S. Environmental Protection Agency and Washington State to serve on the newly formed Hanford Advisory Board suggests that I had achieved some success in this role.

What skills learned in my anthropological career have helped me achieve success outside academia? I attribute my accomplishments to four things: (1) a firm foundation in the concept of culture, which leads one to take a systems approach to problem solving; (2) a relativistic perspective, which leads one to explore alternative ways of doing things as well as to understand why engineers, technocrats, and bureaucrats are the way they are; (3) the epistemology/historiography training received at the University of Pennsylvania, which leads one to question the data assumptions on which decisions are made; and (4) project management skills acquired while managing archaeological projects, which have enabled me to build diverse teams of specialists and accomplish tasks needed to meet specific goals.

The skills acquired since graduate school that have probably helped me most in the nonacademic world are communications related; 90 percent of the problems I encounter at Hanford are communications related, not technical. One need only try to read an anthropology article or hear a presentation at an anthropology conference to realize that **anthropologists need to learn to communicate better if we are going to effectively spread our messages to nonanthropology audiences.**

Thinking about my career, **I do not consider myself as doing anthropology but, rather, as using my anthropology background to**

solve real problems. I firmly believe that if we trained more anthropologists and sent them out to nonanthropological jobs, the world would be better off. The needs and opportunities for transferring anthropological principles from the profession to the workplace are enormous.

Coda

Five years ago I left Battelle to join an engineering firm known as CH2M Hill. There I worked with engineers and local Native Americans to help protect culturally important lands at risk from Hanford Site cleanup activities. Soon after my departure, my wife, Julia Longenecker, went to work in the Cultural Resource Protection Program of the Confederated Tribes of the Umatilla Indian Reservation. The increased contact with Native Americans and exposure to their perspectives toward cultural resources taught us much and transformed our lives in many ways.

In addition to working with Native Americans, I spent a lot of time researching and writing about the history of Hanford plutonium production during the Manhattan Project and the Cold War. The nuclear story is fascinating and one that more anthropologists should explore. There are many lessons that humanity can learn from this chapter of human history.

Recently, in an interesting turn of events, **I returned to Battelle to manage the Hanford Cultural Resources Laboratory for the DOE. Here the job is to protect the resources along the last 51 miles of undammed Columbia River, preserve the history of the Hanford plutonium production mission,** and continue to work with local Indian tribes to identify and protect resources important to them.

In 1997 I was elected to the governing board of NAPA. This was quite an honor and a responsibility. In my original profile, I wrote that the future of anthropology lies outside the academic discipline. I still believe that, and I will continue working to get anthropological perspectives applied more widely across society.

Originally appeared in Anthropology Newsletter, *October 1994*
"Coda" text added, spring 1998 and summer 1999

Practicing Anthropologist, Evaluator, Father?

Michael C. Reed

Science and Mathematics Program Improvement, Western Michigan University

Michael Reed, Marla, and Rachel (age two), summer 1997

The following self-profile was written about four years ago, in the fall–winter of 1995. Since that time, I was "downsized" from the Washington, D.C., job in late March of 1999. Another anthropologist and I were the first two senior people who were let go in a bout of bloodletting as the struggling firm tried to save its skin. (The last I heard, in September 1999, things were grimmer than ever at the firm, and the president was getting desperate enough to [1] bring in an OD consultant and [2] seek out "visionary mission statements" from the remaining skeletal staff.) Losing a job is always shocking, but my wife and I quickly decided that we would turn disappointment into an energetic new adventure. We are now relocated in Kalamazoo, Michigan, where I work on program evaluation (innovative K–12 math and science) for a small, collegial 11-person research group. My family, including two young girls, and I are much happier now. I continue to work on a coedited book on Gabon, Africa, due out in summer 2000 from Westview Press. More and more, I identify myself as an evaluator, and a father, and an Africanist (the latter something of an avocation); the "anthropologist" tag seems less important as time goes on.

So, what does a practicing anthropologist's "career" look like? I was born in Denver, Colorado, in 1951, the oldest of four kids. My mother was a housewife (later an elementary schoolteacher), my father a World War II bomber pilot who made a career in the Air Force. Transient military life led to a succession of childhood homes (in the Philippines; East Lansing, Michigan; Savannah, Georgia; Anchorage, Alaska; and Colorado Springs, Colorado) for my brother, two sisters, and me. Such mobility seemed fun until adolescence, when friendships became both harder to make and harder to break. In addition, I had skipped most of second grade, and I was thereafter younger than most of my classmates.

My undergraduate years (1968–72) at Middlebury College (where I majored in American studies and took no anthropology) were also the time of antiwar protests (even in Vermont's hills), Cream and Joni Mitchell albums, youthful angst, a sister's emerging schizophrenia, and my parents' divorce. Upon graduating, I decided at the last moment not to enter the journalism program at Northwestern University, reasoning that 17 straight years of schooling were enough for now. Thus, I launched into my twenties—bookish and private, filled with vague left-wing ardor, cut off from steadying home ties, and disinterested (for the moment) in career or a family of my own.

For the next seven years I worked as a cook, traveled widely, and wrote about 35 short stories (none ever published). While living in Seattle, graduate school became compelling to me as I was on the heels of a failed romance that left me needful of some new, engrossing future. Several years before, a close friend—who had been my first college professor—had urged me to become an anthropologist. At the time, this advice did not register. The idea came back to me in January 1979 as I hiked across town to the University of Washington's anthropology department, picked up the paperwork, and actually met the application deadline (by a day or two).

Mine was, thus, the epitome of "lack of career planning" (which would later, perhaps fairly enough, frustrate me): this was the only department to which I had applied, and, at that time, I knew nothing about the department's strengths or specialties. My introduction to the anthropological literature began only that spring. As a graduate student, I focused on a geographical area, equatorial Africa, not with any particular prudent foresight but for handy or idiosyncratic reasons (e.g., I had long been fond of Conrad's *Heart of Darkness*; I was intrigued by the French connection; and the department happened to have several Africanists). In 1983, on my second attempt, I won a Fulbright Fellowship and was off, first to France and then to Gabon for 15 months, during which I lived and breathed the rich experience of fieldwork. This involved independent research (on the political economy of a small inland town), francophone African culture, and friendly, humid Gabon. Thirteen years later, I am still savoring and digesting that experience.

Once back from the field, three more years (1985–88) elapsed before I was awarded my Ph.D. In the meantime, I managed one solid (although more historical than anthropological) publication in a reputable British journal. In the end, I didn't really want to leave the university (despite some distaste for what I took to be "petty" departmental politics and the prospect of teaching ANTH 101 again and again). **I had desired an academic career since I was in high school, and I had not given much thought to anything else. However, academic job hunting was fruitless, and I had no stomach for the vagrant, penniless life of a "gypsy scholar."** At the age of 38—short on publications, an Africanist in a society ever more disinterested in Africa, and lacking any "movers and shakers" on my graduate committee—**I essentially abandoned the dream of ever becoming a professor of anthropology.**

In late 1989, following two months of unemployment in southwestern Michigan, I responded to a newspaper job ad and found work (salary: $27,000) with a university research center specializing in program evaluation. **For me, evaluation lacked anthropology's rich history and theory, but it did offer practical contact with fascinating social research efforts.** Unfortunately, three years at this center did little to develop my anthropological skills or professional self-identity (although I was hired as an "anthropologist," this role was never encouraged). **Although I found American Evaluation Association annual meetings to be small and friendly, my attempts to collaborate with professional evaluators just never "clicked."** Perhaps many of us anthropologists tend to remain even more "marginal" than we might like.

By 1992, I yearned for "bright lights"; I wanted a respectable salary, and I wanted to be an anthropologist once again. An ad in *The Chronicle of Higher Education* sought "part-time consultant ethnographers" to do federal contract work. I applied and, a couple of weeks later, received a phone call from the president of a Washington, D.C., research firm inviting me to come interview for a full-time position. I was offered a job on the spot, accepted, gave notice, rented a Ryder truck, got married, drove to Washington, and started work the following Monday in October 1992.

I am now one among perhaps 25 Ph.D.s working for a private, for-profit research and evaluation firm in downtown D.C. that conducts and evaluates federal contract research. The firm, which first earned its spurs in the Head Start field in the late 1960s and early 1970s, now has about 110 employees and contracts with several federal agencies including the Office of National Drug Control Policy and the National Institute of Justice. Mine is a specialized but multifaceted niche in the firm: I am a methodologist, an "anthropologist," a "qualitative" analyst, an advocate of creating (and analyzing) verbatim focus group transcripts; I "know" text-analysis software (e.g., askSam, NUD*IST); I organize and write proposals; I conduct site visits; and I am a proponent of "fourth generation"–style evaluation. By temperament and interest, I seem to be less of an up-front manager and more of a task-oriented researcher and writer.

Despite the late start, twists and turns, and occasional disappointments in my practicing anthropological career, I now am often gratified to be able to *think like and work as an anthropologist.* In recent years I have become increasingly involved with the American Anthropological Association and NAPA as well as with the Society for Applied Anthropology. **I maintain active and collegial ties with other applied and practicing anthropologists. Among my colleagues at the research firm, I am aware of no other academic discipline (e.g., sociology, psychology, education) that fosters the sort of *disciplinary self-identity, collaborative work habits, and theoretical inquisitiveness found among anthropologists.*** I do believe we are a breed apart, and we need to continue to work hard to build on such strengths.

The more I study anthropology and its history, the more I believe that academia is merely one (and a late-arriving one at that) venue of activity. Pre-Boasian anthropologists (with or without Ph.D.s) were a fascinating lot—people of letters, inspired amateurs, government employees, missionaries, museum workers, and wacky bon vivants (such as Frank Cushing). Franz Boas insisted that anthropology *credentialize* and *professionalize* and thereby squeezed out many talented (and nonconformist) people, effectively narrowing anthropology into a university-based discipline. In time, our roots in natural history and the humanities were lost (much to the chagrin of A. Kroeber), and "social science" came to predominate. The past only complicates anthropology's too-easy assumptions of today.

In the end, though, I am a practicing anthropologist by default: I do it because my anticipated academic career did not work out but I still wanted to try to remain a professional anthropologist. (Some of this history is spelled out in a volume that I recently edited, *Practicing Anthropology in a Postmodern World: Lessons and Insights from Federal Contract Research* [1997].) **My personal experience demonstrates that trying to practice anthropology in the private sector is often not easy and not very marketable. By all means, do it if you are committed to being an anthropologist, but be prepared for some professional isolation, some unachieved status, and the need to relish personal satisfactions** (e.g., I'm going back only now to write up field notes into some publishable articles).

Reference Cited

Reed, Michael C., ed.
  1997 Practicing Anthropology in a Postmodern World: Lessons and Insights from Federal Contract Research. NAPA Bulletin, 17. Arlington, VA: American Anthropological Association.

Originally appeared in Anthropology Newsletter, *February 1996*
Revised, spring 1998 and summer 1999

From the Desert of Southeastern Idaho to the Consulting World of the East Coast

Daniel G. Roberts
John Milner Associates, Inc.

My interest in archaeology began in 1959 or 1960, when I was about 12 years old and my parents took me for a visit to the University Museum at the University of Pennsylvania. This was my first encounter with an archaeological museum, and I became enamored, in particular, of the displays in the Egyptian Gallery. As fate would have it, of course, this was as close as I was to get to things Egyptian.

My undergraduate training took place in the "counterculture years" of the late 1960s at Beloit College, a small, liberal arts campus in southern Wisconsin. Why Beloit? Well, at the time, it was one of the preeminent small colleges in the United States for the study of anthropology and archaeology—it still is—and I wanted no part of a large university. **During my Beloit years I had no idea what I was going to do with a career in archaeology** (my interests never leaned toward any of the other anthropological subfields), but I was pretty sure teaching was not something in which I had a strong interest. **Looking back, I suppose I thought I would probably wind up in a museum somewhere as a curator.**

While still an undergraduate, Congress passed the **National Historic Preservation Act in 1966, an event that ultimately was to greatly influence the career paths of many archaeologists, including me. This legislation has been responsible for the creation of thousands of jobs outside the academy** in the fields of archaeology, history, architectural history, historic architecture, and landscape architecture, among others. As a result of the passage of this act, the professional in each of these fields now has the opportunity for employment in private consulting firms and government agencies at the federal, state, and local levels, as well as in museums and teaching.

My career path ultimately led me to the consulting world, when I joined John Milner Associates, Inc. (JMA) in 1976. Before that, however, I obtained my master's degree in early 1976 at Idaho State University (ISU). During my undergraduate years, I became interested in lithic technology but never had the opportunity to get practical experience in it at Beloit. The appeal of studying with Don Crabtree at ISU was great. So I left my familiar surroundings east of the Mississippi and enrolled in the anthropology program leading to the master's degree at ISU in the summer of 1974. Regrettably,

I only got to work with Crabtree briefly, for he became ill and unable to knap stone shortly after my arrival. However, I was fortunate to study under the direction of B. Robert Butler, who graciously supported me with a two-year graduate assistantship. **Little did I know at the time, but that assistantship was to significantly shape my career in archaeology.** Butler had instituted what was probably the first program in applied archaeology in North America, a program in which students were assigned to carry out research leading to the master's degree under the mandates of government contracts and in compliance with Section 106 of the National Historic Preservation Act. My contract work was a two-year sample survey of approximately 275,000 acres of Bureau of Land Management (BLM) land in southeastern Idaho, just west of the Teton Range. **Being responsible for nearly all aspects of this contract, from devising the research design and sampling strategy, supervising a small crew that carried out the fieldwork, conducting the analysis, and preparing the report to making land management recommendations to the BLM was an extremely useful experience that was instrumental in preparing me for the career I was to embark on at JMA immediately after graduation.**

What it did not prepare me for at JMA was the extent to which I would become involved in historical archaeology. All of my archaeological training (at Beloit and ISU) was in various aspects of the prehistory of North America. Indeed, after completion of my thesis on the southeastern Idaho survey, I fancied myself a specialist in the prehistory of the northern Great Basin. But here I was, back in the East in suburban Philadelphia, a scant 35 miles from where I grew up, and the third archaeologist to be hired at what was at the time primarily an architectural restoration firm. In the mid-1970s, the firm was heavily engaged in local and regional restorations of historical properties or landmarks, and the architects frequently needed below-ground assistance that would provide clues to aid in restoration. Indeed, I am convinced that, at the time, the architects believed that this kind of work was what archaeologists were principally trained to do! **I disparagingly referred to this work as "porch-footing archaeology" because it seemed that all the architects usually wanted us to find were the locations of former porch footings.**

Fortunately, the firm's owners at the time allowed the archaeologists enough latitude to begin to seek their own contracts—and that is precisely what we began to do. In short order we obtained archaeological contracts with the National Park Service, the State of Maryland, the Pennsylvania Department of Transportation, and several other private and government entities. Soon, the Archaeology Department expanded significantly, becoming the Cultural Resources Department, and included not only archaeologists but also historians and architectural historians. I became director of the Cultural Resources Department in 1983 and a major shareholder of the firm in 1986, and today, the Cultural Resources Department accounts for approximately 60 percent of JMA's business volume.

My job for the past 20 years or so can best be described as archae-ological administration. Indeed, I have not been in the field other than to visit ongoing projects since 1980, and I have not singly authored an archae-ological compliance report since about the same time. I have, however, coauthored many compliance reports and publications, normally as a junior author to the principal investigator's senior authorship (JMA's Cultural Re-sources Department has more than 20 Ph.D.– and M.A.–level professionals who are responsible for the implementation, conduct, and completion of proj-ects, from the proposal through the report preparation stages). My responsi-bilities center on the general operation of the department, including personnel assignments, personnel actions, contract negotiations, marketing and sales, legal matters, quality assurance and control, and corporate policy decision making as a member of JMA's five-person Board of Directors.

With the benefit of hindsight, I can see that my training at Beloit Col-lege and ISU prepared me reasonably well for the path my career ulti-mately was to take. However, I must emphasize that **by far the most use-ful aspects of that training were the practical, applied experiences** that I had. At Beloit, that experience centered on gaining firsthand expertise in the techniques of archaeological fieldwork in an intensive, summer-long field school at several late prehistoric sites in northern Wisconsin; and at ISU, it centered on the experience gained by being directly responsible for the successful completion of a long-term government contract. Certainly the more traditional classroom aspects of my training were not without benefit, for it was there, of course, that the groundwork was laid for my knowledge of archaeological method and theory. But my training afforded me absolutely no background in such skills as contract negotiation, dis-pute resolution, client-consultant relations, cost accounting, budgeting, personnel matters, legal issues, liability insurance, or professional ethics, to name only a few. Any expertise I now have in each of these areas came from on-the-job experience and, in many cases, trial by fire.

The world of private industry cultural resources consulting is rife with challenges every day, and after more than 23 years in this industry, the various twists, turns, and permutations of those challenges have never ceased to amaze me. But the **overarching challenge that I have always tried to meet is to combine sound and ethical business practices with the provision of high-quality professional services and products to clients**—products and services that not only will achieve client objectives but will also favorably withstand professional scrutiny. Without a combina-tion of both, the cultural resources consultant will likely not achieve the measure of success or satisfaction that may be desired.

New entry, spring 1998
Revised, summer 1999

Applied Anthropology in the Management of Native American Cultural Resources: Archaeology, Ethnography, and History of Traditional Cultural Places

T. J. Ferguson
Heritage Resources Management Consultants

I practice a form of **applied anthropology that integrates archaeology, ethnography, and ethnohistoric research** to collect the information needed to manage Native Americans' cultural resources. Today most of my work is done as a consultant under contract to Indian tribes that set the research agenda, participate in the collection and analysis of data, and control the work product. This research entails both **exciting research opportunities and challenging ethical obligations.**

At the beginning of my career, after completing a master's degree in anthropology at the University of Arizona, I was hired by the Pueblo of Zuni to help develop one of the first tribally based cultural resource management programs in the United States. As Tribal Archaeologist, I advised the Zuni Tribal Council on the management of cultural resources, but most of my job responsibilities entailed conducting conventional archaeological surveys and excavations under contract to federal agencies, fulfilling their responsibilities pursuant to the National Historic Preservation Act.

After several years, Pueblo leaders asked me to assist them with efforts to repatriate Zuni War Gods (sacred artifacts that had been stolen from shrines on Zuni land) and to interview tribal elders to collect information needed to litigate land claims against the U.S. government. Both of these assignments required the application of ethnographic and ethnohistoric approaches that expanded my professional work beyond archaeology. I became interested in the ethnography of archaeological sites, that is, studying how archaeological sites and historic places function as cultural properties used in the retention and transmission of traditional Native American cultures. **My work began to focus on integrating archaeology, ethnography, and historical research to study the significance of places and landscapes in the living history of contemporary peoples.**

After working for the Pueblo of Zuni for six years, I returned to graduate school at the University of New Mexico to earn both a master's degree in community and regional planning and a Ph.D. in anthropology. During this period, I pursued my research interests while employed by the Institute of the North American West, a nonprofit educational corporation. Today

I own and operate Heritage Resources Management Consultants, a business partnership with Roger Anyon. The focus of our business is providing a wide range of research and management services to tribes in the Southwest, although we occasionally work for museums, federal agencies, and companies in the private sector.

My formal anthropological education has served me well during my career. The University of Arizona stressed a **four-field anthropological curriculum** that provided me with the knowledge I later needed when my interests expanded beyond archaeological study of the past. A solid foundation in ethnology, biological anthropology, and linguistics allowed me to develop my professional skills as needed in the context of specific projects. My course work for the Ph.D. at the University of New Mexico was more intensively focused on developing the archaeological method and theory needed to understand the creation, use, and deposition of material culture in the archaeological record and to relate these to broad problems of human behavior and culture.

The fundamental field skills learned in archaeological training are very helpful in my work, much of which entails the precise location and description of traditional cultural properties. An archaeological perspective incorporating materialist as well as cultural variables is essential in understanding the persistence of these historic places. The evaluation of these traditional cultural properties, however, requires that ethnographic and historical information be considered in addition to physical attributes. **To be done well, this work must be undertaken in close collaboration with the Native Americans who use the traditional cultural properties.**

Many Native Americans are antagonistic toward scholarly research because they feel that their cultures have been violated by publications that divulge esoteric information. Therefore, I structure my work so that the tribes I work for make the decisions about what information to reveal and to whom it will be revealed. The fact that I have consciously not learned the languages of the people I work for creates a situation in which I must collaborate with native speakers in the research and reports I produce. This means that **my Native American clients remain the cultural experts,** and my role is essentially that of a facilitator and amanuensis rather than an advocate. I simply try to help people explain their cultural concerns in a manner that effectively communicates with the state and federal agencies that regulate historic preservation.

In this work, there is an ethical obligation to conduct research that both meets project objectives and is congruent with tribal cultural values. **The ethics of this research are challenging because they are constantly evolving as the tribes gain a better understanding of scholarly research and historic preservation.** There are many unresolved issues that complicate the situation. For instance, my professional ethic to share what I learn with my colleagues is often at odds with tribal ethics to keep esoteric information from being divulged to outsiders. This and other potential conflicts in research are minimized by carefully constructed contracts that require reports and publications to undergo tribal review. My contracted research is a work for hire, and the tribes I work for therefore own my work products. These tribes graciously allow me to publish some aspects of my work, and the review that precedes this is always helpful in making sure my perspectives accurately reflect tribal knowledge and concerns.

My formal anthropological education has prepared me well for the research I do. The **one area I wish I had more formal training in is basic business management.** Contracted research requires careful budgeting of time and money, and I had to learn the fundamentals of management and accounting on the job. Although I have learned what I need to know, formal training in business management would have facilitated the development of my career.

I find the applied anthropology I do as a livelihood to be very satisfying. I enjoy helping tribal leaders and elders effectively interact with land managing agencies and historic preservation regulators. My work continually takes me to interesting places, and I am personally enriched by the history Native Americans choose to share with me. **Running my own small business gives me the personal flexibility I want to pursue the self-funded archaeological research that interests me** while at the same time working on a wider range of contracted research projects. It feels good to conduct research that the people I am studying find useful for their own ends and, at the same time, contributes to a greater anthropological understanding of past and present peoples.

New entry, spring 1998 and summer 1999

You Gotta Have Friends

Cathleen Crain and Nathaniel (Niel) Tashima
LTG Associates, Inc.

About Cathleen and Niel

I am he as you are he as you are me and we are all together.

—"I Am the Walrus," Paul McCartney and John Lennon, 1967

We began LTG Associates as colleagues and friends, and we have worked as a team for the past 18 years. LTG was created by the two of us as a vehicle so that we could apply our skills, training, and experience in situations that intrigued us. As an 18-year-old, woman- and minority-owned consulting firm, we have worked in community development and program and policy evaluation at the local, state, and federal levels. We are the managing partners and are ultimately responsible for the work and products of the company. That is the easy part of the profile.

One of the early realizations for each of us was that working together enhanced our enjoyment of the work and gave us an opportunity to explore how anthropology related to a variety of interests. We also discovered very early on that we worked very well as a team. How does one describe the wonderful opportunity to push the science of our discipline as well as the creative application of anthropology while having a good time? The qualifier is that **a great deal of the time has been spent administering a business, developing contracts, and working with personnel issues—in short, developing the infrastructure and staff to support the work of the company.** This has also meant that we have been constantly learning: learning how to manage a business; learning how to develop contracts and business; learning how to use anthropology in diverse settings; learning how to manage, mentor, and train staff for both corporate functions and the research and analysis that is the lifeblood of the organization.

Niel Tashima is a fourth-generation Japanese American from a small Central Valley town in California. He had ambitions in the hard sciences in his early years, nurtured by a faulty stereotype of Asian Americans. He received his B.A. from the University of California, San Diego, his M.A. from San Diego State University, and his Ph.D. at Northwestern University. His graduate work at Northwestern was under the tutelage of first Francis L. K. Hsu and then Oswald Werner. Niel's academic anthropology experience was focused on psychological anthropology with a strong four-field grounding. Throughout his academic training, he was involved in other pursuits, which have colored some of his application of anthropology in the real world. **Working as a high school football coach taught Niel a great deal about motivation and intestinal fortitude as well as teamwork.** His work in community organizing provided rich experiences in how communities coalesce, define themselves, and then take action. Finally, his work in mental health created opportunities to observe how systems operate and the essential nature of culture.

Cathleen Crain is multiethnic, Anglo-American and Cherokee, from the San Francisco Bay area. She had ambitions in medicine in her early years, before being seduced by anthropology with the promise of being able to change the culture of institutions and systems. She completed her education (B.A. with honors and M.A.) at McMaster University in Hamilton, Ontario, Canada. Strongly supported in her professional aspirations by a traditional four-field program, Cathleen eschewed further graduate training to launch herself into applying her skills. Throughout her career, she has worked to change systems so that they are more responsive, acceptable, and accountable to the people they are intended to serve. Her early experiences as a hospital volunteer, counselor for disabled children, and foster parent have all influenced the manner in which she has applied her anthropological training. Her job as the first anthropologist/therapist in a regional rehabilitation hospital was marked by her work in creating systems and a real role for anthropological tools in the assessment of client needs, development of treatment plans, and provision of culturally appropriate treatment. Before creating LTG, Cathleen was the director of a health enabling service with a staff of 30, representing 15 different languages and dialects, and then the director of services for a national private voluntary organization.

We spend most of our work lives "coast-shifting" between LTG staffs and offices in California and Washington, D.C. (which is not a life to be recommended for anyone who wishes to maintain sanity). We have defined *coast-shifting* as the art of moving from California to D.C. on a regular basis with minimal psychic and paper dislocation. On the one hand it is fraught with difficulties: Where did I leave that disk? Where are those field notes? Who is directing this project? At the same time, the cultural contexts of the two communities, rural California versus metropolitan Washington, present wonderful opportunities to see and experience the world through very different lenses.

Through its work, LTG has been a fascinating **laboratory to test anthropological methods and theory in real world applications.** It has also been a challenge learning to run a company while at the same time maintaining high standards of ethics, research methods, and community perspectives. We believe that striving for a state of dynamic equilibrium is the optimal status. No matter where in the business we direct our attention, we (and the business) are always in motion. Communities we work with are always changing. Government and private sector needs are in a constant state of flux. Finally, anthropology as a discipline is also changing. Our challenge has been to keep up to date with the multitude of issues.

LTG Associates, Inc., focuses on research, evaluation, program development, and policy analysis in health and human services, with a special focus on issues of access to services. In addition, facilitation, management consultation, and community organizing are areas of skill and interest, contributing to the design of products and the contextualization of research findings. Anthropology is valued in the LTG workplace and in the projects developed by the company. LTG has employed as staff or engaged as consultants dozens of anthropologists across the country. The company today is larger, far more sophisticated, and more complex than the mom-and-pop operation that began 18 years ago. The early years of the firm focused on projects in which the two of us were the major staff. As the company has grown, both of us have assumed more administrative and development activities and have less field time. The loss of direct field time has been balanced by the opportunity to work with teams of anthropologists and other professionals. However, the trade of field time for desk time has not been a happy one: we miss the experience and struggle to remain fresh and connected to the field.

From its beginning, the firm has been involved in a wide variety of projects. For example, LTG has been involved in HIV/AIDS–related work since 1987. **Our HIV/AIDS work has taken us from clinical facilities to the streets of communities at risk.** We have worked with senior program managers in the Ryan White Care Program, as well as outreach workers in most of the major metropolitan areas of the United States. LTG was invited by a number of Southeast Asian refugee communities to work with them during the early years of their development. **In working with Southeast Asian communities throughout California, LTG was directly involved in assisting these developing communities with understanding how U.S. government and community cultures operate.** LTG provided assistance to these communities in organizational development, project design, and cultural brokering among the various concerned parties. Tuberculosis was a focus of two projects over four years, and LTG developed important information that has helped to shape services to those infected and at risk.

Other issues in which LTG has been active include hepatitis, homelessness, mental health, substance abuse, child abuse and neglect, foster care and adoption, the space station program, and food security. For the past three years LTG has helped lay the groundwork for the development of geriatric policy and programs. **Most recently, LTG became the home for monitoring and evaluation of USAID maternal child health, child survival, and nutrition programs worldwide. LTG has worked in all 50 states, in every U.S.–affiliated territory except the Virgin Islands, and with over 35 ethnic communities in the United States.**

LTG began with and continues to focus on the use of qualitative methods. However, the use of quantitative methods is an important aspect of LTG work today. Examples of quantitative projects include the gathering and analysis of national adoption and foster care data and population outreach and survey work in support of radioactive dose reconstruction efforts in eastern Washington.

In each of these issues, whatever the project, LTG has brought a distinctly anthropological voice to the table, whether or not anthropology was expected or recognized. LTG has taken the tools of anthropology and used them to affect the shape of policy, programs, and the impact that services have on people's lives. In every project that LTG has successfully completed, there have been common elements. The first is that a team has worked together and has allowed the project to exceed the talents and experience of any of the individuals involved. A second element has been a **clear focus on method, with the method and its application being accessible both to the team and to those participating in and receiving the outcomes of the work.**

Our work has taken us and the company from the design and implementation of agricultural training projects for Hmong refugees to providing interactive, topically localized evaluation seminars for ministries and departments of health in the associated states and territories of the United States in the Pacific. The LTG application of anthropological methods has ranged from HIV outreach and education in the South Bronx to identifying cultural issues of concern for multicultural crews of a space station. LTG has worked in program development from the local county level to that of federal agencies and bureaus. Its work has encompassed most of the major public health agencies in the U.S. federal government.

We believe that in order to move anthropology forward, it is critical to be actively involved in the life of the discipline, especially around issues of professional anthropology. We both have been active in the past in local practitioner organizations and are fellows in the Society for Applied Anthropology. For the past decade, much of our discipline-based work has focused on activities involving the American Anthropological Association (AAA). In 1987 Niel coauthored the NAPA "Statement on Ethics" with Claudia Fishman and M. Jean Gilbert. Niel was treasurer of NAPA for two terms and is a past president of NAPA. He has been appointed to the Finance Committee for AAA. Cathleen cochaired the NAPA Mentor Committee with Madeline Iris and was chair of the NAPA Toolkit Committee. In addition, Niel and Cathleen cochair the AAA Professional Development Committee, looking at development of continuing education for professional anthropologists. Cathleen also was appointed to the Committee on the Status of Women of the AAA as the first professional anthropologist on the committee; there is now a permanent elective seat on the committee for professional anthropology. We conduct the annual NAPA practicum on professional ethics at the AAA meeting, an interactive forum to explore ethical dilemmas for professional anthropologists.

LTG encourages all of its professionals to be active in discipline-focused organizations, in the belief that it is enriching to the individual, the discipline, and the company. In addition to organizational involvement, we and other LTG professional staff regularly talk with students and new professionals about careers in anthropology. **It is essential that professionals both engage in the discipline and nurture younger anthropologists as they seek their professional identity.**

Part of the pleasure of working in LTG has been to engage with other anthropologists to focus and magnify our skills through our work as teams. LTG also affords the opportunity to be curious about almost everything that has to do with the human condition. The major satisfaction in LTG work is in the positive outcomes for people and systems in critical areas of health and human services.

The challenges presented in the profession of anthropology are exciting and engaging. As we look into the future, we see an increasingly complex and interactive world demanding more flexibility and creativity from all of us. We believe anthropology has the tools to clearly articulate the problems and issues faced by communities and institutions and to collaborate in the development of appropriate solutions.

Originally appeared in Anthropology Newsletter, *October 1993*
Revised, spring 1998 and summer 1999

Challenging a Paradigm in Two Directions: Anthropologists in Business and the Business of Practicing Anthropology

Judith Benson

Judith Benson
Boeing Co.

Preparation

Two outstanding events during my doctoral studies at the University of California at Los Angeles (UCLA) reflected the direction of my future work. The first was when the chairman of my doctoral committee told me that I was "a mile wide and an inch thin." What his comment meant to me was that I lacked the depth of involvement in a single topic so important in classical ethnography. The second was the difficulty I had in obtaining approval for my doctoral topic. The doctoral topic I selected was an anthropological evaluation of the national Peruvian traditional birth attendant program. As I recall, the primary objection was to the lack of "theory" in my approach. Opposition to my topic ended when I received my contract from USAID to do this work, supplemented by a large dollar grant from Occidental Petroleum. At the time, **I had absolutely no idea where my practical, applied, multidimensional approach fit into anthropology. I just knew that it made sense to me.** At that point in my career, I thought I needed support from my university sponsors. I was under the impression that their opinion of me and my work could influence my career in anthropology. I understood how important letters of recommendation, informal networking, and "the old-boys network" were to being able to get a coveted faculty position at a university when I completed my doctoral work. At that time, that was the only line of work I really understood was possible.

However, that career path was not in my stars at that point in time. There was a wide gap between my paradigm of how anthropologists practice their profession and the prevailing ideas within my department. From a very early point in my graduate work, my own criteria for selecting work topics were based on whether a task or activity resulted in a product that had value for someone or something.

When I think about it, **I have reinvented myself many times.** My undergraduate work at UCLA was in microbiology, and I started my professional life as a medical technologist. This lasted until my first child was born two weeks before I received my undergraduate degree. I took the next ten years off, devoting my time entirely to child raising. My interest in anthropology was kindled as a result of a lecture given by Johannes Wilbert on shamanism. I was fascinated by the subject and decided right then and there that I wanted to do my graduate work in anthropology. For some reason, far too distant to remember, I ended up with a master's degree in archaeology from California State University at Northridge. My master's topic was an interpretation of a pre-Hispanic Peruvian ceramic motif. While doing fieldwork for my master's thesis in Peru, I renewed my interest in traditional medicine. With the support of Barbara Meyerhoff (who served as my informal mentor), I was introduced to Wilbert. He was the chairman of her doctoral committee. He accepted me as a graduate student, and, thus, I began my doctoral work at UCLA.

During my graduate studies at UCLA, I continued to follow my interest in traditional medicine and, with the assistance of the Tinker Foundation, studied the survival of traditional medicine in *barriadas* (low-income communities on the outskirts of large Latin American cities) on the north coast and in northern highlands of Peru. My doctoral dissertation topic came about as a result of informal conversations with Peruvian health officials and members of the Peruvian health community I knew from the time I was in Peru doing work for my master's thesis. During these conversations, I discovered that the traditional birth attendant training program was an important part of the national primary health care initiative and that it had never been formally evaluated. The fact that this national program was taught to individuals all across the various ethnographic zones of Peru fascinated me because it meant that I would be able to examine how underlying beliefs, customs, and so on influenced the program's outcome.

The Bridge

After completing my doctoral work, I continued to work on various consulting contracts for USAID. At the same time I decided to begin a Master's of Public Health (MPH) degree at the School of Public Health at UCLA. I really was not sure what I wanted to do, and I thought an MPH made sense. I spent a year in the health services division. That year was pivotal for me. Two classes have influenced me to this day: one was "Strategic Planning"; the other was "Small Area Planning." The appeal of both of these was their practical and rational approach to health care. I also further realized that a degree in public health would not benefit the direction I wanted to take: I needed to get out of school and find out about the real world.

The Private Sector—Health Care

Based on my background in health care and interest in strategic planning, I looked for a job in the classified ads in my local newspaper under "health care." As one can well imagine, it did not take me long to realize that I needed to develop a résumé and that my publications, grants, and academic awards did not hold much currency in the job market in which I now found myself. **After I figured out how to market myself, I got a few job offers.** One was from Kaiser Permanente, and another was from St. Vincent's Hospital. Based on my view of the world at that time, I picked the job with the biggest salary and nicest office.

After I had spent six months at St. Vincent's Hospital, it did not take too much effort for my former professor at the School of Public Health to convince me to leave and come to work for her at the Center for Health Management Research. My job was to develop research proposals to keep the center afloat. I came up with some innovative proposals that focused on ethnicity and response to health care. I was particularly interested in compliance in ethnic populations with diabetes and hypertension. Unfortunately, none of my proposals was funded, and soon the center was short on money. During my time at the center, I became fascinated with the response of the Hispanic elderly population to managed health care. The center was sponsored by the Lutheran Hospital Society, now Unihealth. PacifiCare was also part of this network. I successfully marketed my proposal to study the response of elderly Hispanics to managed care to PacifiCare. When the study was completed, I returned to the classified ads and came up with a job at Children's Hospital in Los Angeles, to do satisfaction surveys and market research. Political upheavals led to my supervisor losing her job and a rather unstable work environment. I had maintained contact with the individual who had initially offered me the job at Kaiser Permanente and he was still interested.

For seven years I worked at Kaiser Permanente in the Member Services Department. At the same time, I took classes at UCLA Extension, leading to certificates in Total Quality Management (TQM) and systems analysis. **My responsibilities at Kaiser ranged from setting up a computerized system for the documentation of complaints and grievances to group facilitation, local call center management, focus groups, training, financial management, TQM, and organizational development.** I was also involved in the development of a regional call center that was part of a large scale re-engineering effort led by Deloitte-Touche. It was clear to me that upon its completion, my job would change so radically that it would no longer interest me. After some informal networking, I located a very interesting position with a two-year re-engineering project that was to be conducted by a joint Kaiser–Andersen Consulting team. The position I took was Change Management Team Leader. It was absolutely wonderful! I learned from the Andersen team, and they learned from me.

Kathryn Stevens, the project director, hired me specifically because I was a cultural anthropologist. It is instructive to take a look at what that meant for the project. This is described as follows:

When Kathryn Stevens of Kaiser Permanente Southern California Region re-
quested permission to hire a cultural anthropologist, few of her colleagues
grasped the reason. A cultural anthropologist? But Stevens . . . had a simple
explanation for the doubters: The anthropologist's perspective enhances
team member's understanding of how best to implement improved processes
in a way that affected employees can sustain a cultural change. [Jennings et
al. 1997:253]

During the year and a half that I worked for Kathryn, I smoothed the
way for process change by providing guidance to team members on how
to identify the cultural context within which the change would take place. I
worked closely with individuals whom I recognized as potential roadblocks
to the process change. I tried to stay away from the term *resisters* because
that seemed so negative. I spent time with these major stakeholders to understand their points of view. At the same time, **I worked with team members so that they could develop the process change in a way that
blended with rather than confronted the existing cultural context.**
Among my accomplishments as part of the team, perhaps the most
graphic was my development of a series of interventions that provided opportunities for communication, idea sharing, and collaboration. These happened through site visits, video conferencing, and mediated visits.

As the project began to wind down, I questioned whether there was a
continued match between the direction I was going in and the direction
Kaiser Permanente was taking at that time. The Human Resources Department was in the process of being reorganized, and I thought it wise to
move out of Kaiser. Perhaps I was looking for new and untouched pastures
to graze in.

Private Sector—Aerospace

Currently I am working in Long Beach, California, as a senior organizational development consultant at Douglas Products Division, part of the
Boeing Company. Again, **my background as an anthropologist appeals
tremendously to the client population, whether they are shop floor
mechanics, vice presidents, or senior managers.** They see my background as an important ingredient in efforts to facilitate cultural change.
My primary responsibilities are the design and implementation of change
strategies.

The first project I engaged myself in was an analysis of the cultural
context of the workplace. From the shop floor, to middle management, and
then to upper management, I explored how things are done and the glue
that holds it all together. Examples are my involvement with self-directed
work teams (SDWTs) and integrated product teams (IPTs). A small group
of SDWTs were formed a year ago as a pilot. As a result, great strides have
been made in the reduction of cycle time and the corresponding decrease
in unit cost in these areas. However, while the focus has been on team

leader training, there has been little understanding of how this impacts the work life of shop floor mechanics. By interviewing shop floor mechanics in one unit, I have been able to develop and recommend changes in the way team leaders work with their groups so that the process will come closer to its theoretical intent—the involvement of the whole labor force in determining the course of work.

My involvement with IPTs continues to be as a mediator and translator between and within functional areas. One of the challenges in improving operational effectiveness and efficiency is reduction in time span and operating cost. When individuals from different functions are not working toward common goals or do not understand the upstream and downstream impact of their decisions regarding a work effort, valuable time, materials, and energy can be lost. My task over the last year has been supporting the leadership in its efforts to align the organization toward common goals.

Looking back on the 15 years since I completed my doctorate, I find myself continually renewed and fascinated by the process of conducting applied anthropology work in business environments. My continual challenge is to create linkages within the workplace to contribute to greater work satisfaction while at the same time meeting business objectives.

Reference Cited

Jennings, Ken, Kurt Miller, and Sharyn Materna
    1997 Changing Health Care: Creating Tomorrow's Winning Health Enterprise Today. Santa Monica: Knowledge Exchange.

Originally appeared in Anthropology Newsletter, *November 1996*
Revised, spring 1998 and summer 1999

Communicating Anthropology

Dawn Bodo
Kids Korps USA

On that November day in 1988 when I informed my manager, the vice president of a large communications company, that I was leaving "the Business" to become an anthropologist, his facial expression revealed his opinion: "Is this woman crazy? **What person in her right mind would leave a high-paying, high-profile job for some low-paying, obscure career?**" Some of my colleagues believed my unstable condition was the result of 22 years of exceedingly long hours and grinding deadlines. I must admit that those same thoughts also had crossed my mind.

I first became interested in anthropology in 1987. My professor, Dr. John Gutowski, "wowed" me with colorful accounts of anthropologists' fieldwork in remote areas of the world—of languages, rituals, and belief systems so different from my own. I was hooked. Soon, however, my practical side got the best of me: How could I, a 39-year-old mother and step-mother of six teenagers working and living in suburban Detroit, afford to become an anthropologist? Surely there must be a way to apply anthropological knowledge and skills without having to leave the country—or even the state.

My answer came when I noticed a newspaper article featuring Dr. Marietta Baba, a corporate anthropologist and professor of anthropology at Wayne State University in Detroit. **Eureka! Anthropologists DO work in business settings. They work at General Motors Corporation, the Upjohn Company, Proctor and Gamble Company, and Westinghouse.** Within an hour, I was on the phone with Dr. Baba. Shortly thereafter, I entered her Business Anthropology Program.

On the day I left the communications business, I gathered all my communications artifacts: art supplies, books, videos, business proposals, correspondences, and portfolio. In my mind, they soon would be remnants of a career past. In the years to come, however, I would discover that the skill set I developed in one career transferred remarkably well into another. The "on-the-job" knowledge and skills I gained as an artist, writer, and producer have proven to be indispensable in building my career as an anthropologist.

In the communications industry, I wrote business proposals to, and developed budgets and program plans for, executives of Fortune 500 companies; designed slide presentations for national corporate meetings;

and produced marketing materials and training videos for diverse audiences. **In short, I learned how to communicate to a lay audience—an important skill.** Applied anthropologists may be asked to write grants; communicate their findings—orally and visually—to managers, clients, or employers; and train people in communities to continue the work they started together.

Learning how to work effectively with multidisciplinary teams and to manage multiple projects were two other important skills I learned in my first career. As a creative director and manager of an audiovisual department, I learned how to bring together people from different "subcultures"—artists, writers, photographers, and salespeople—for the purpose of developing and implementing quality projects. The communications world has its own language, subgroups, rituals, and a wide range of attitudes, beliefs, and behaviors. **I often had to act as the culture broker between two work groups with different opinions and ways of doing things.** The same kind of brokering or translating of skills is needed by anthropologists who work with communities, businesses, and organizations.

I learned that teamwork is more than just working together and sharing ideas. Listening, acknowledging others' accomplishments and ideas, and making positive use of constructive criticism are essential to team dynamics; these skills can critically influence the quality of a final product. An inferior product—characterized by missed deadlines, budget overages, and poor quality—ultimately may result in lost business and jobs. For the same reasons, teamwork is an important component of anthropological work, whether the team members are protecting archaeological sites, organizing community outreach programs, coauthoring articles or books, designing new college courses, or implementing new programs in the workplace. **Communications skills must not be taken for granted; they are critical to the development and maintenance of long-term relationships among individuals, groups, and communities.**

The skill set I developed in my former career enabled me to embrace anthropological work in a unique way. I designed and conducted a customer satisfaction study for an advertising agency serving Fortune 500 clients, conducted a study to identify communications issues between an American manufacturing company and its Canadian and Mexican clients, investigated employee issues associated with corporate restructuring, conducted a study for an automotive company to identify sales skills training needs, and worked with a multidisciplinary sociotechnical systems team that investigated the impact of work culture on the implementation of new technology in a corporation and military base.

When I left the communications industry, I was certain that I would never write and produce another video. I was wrong again. During a visit to Northern Arizona University, I met Dr. Cathy Small, a professor who was working with Native American craftspeople to establish an economic cooperative. One of her project goals was to document Southwest

Indian arts and artists for the purpose of educating the public about the work of Navajo, Zuni, and Hopi artists and their concerns about copycat art. Opportunity! Four months later I was standing with a Navajo videographer in a small shop on the reservation interviewing a Hopi craftsman about the spiritual value of his work.

By combining my communications and anthropological knowledge and skills, a whole new arena of work was possible. A few months after completing *Of Hands and Hearts: Southwest Indian Arts and Artists,* **Dr. Elizabeth Briody and I began planning a video about careers in applied anthropology entitled *Anthropologists at Work: Careers Making a Difference.*** The most exciting part of co-producing the video was the opportunity to work with, and learn from, anthropologists who have their own unique skill sets—skills that, like mine, have developed through experience and time.

I realize, more than ever, the importance of integrating one's personal interests, knowledge, and skills both in building a rewarding career and in manifesting one's life vision. Twenty-nine years of work experience enabled me to establish a nonprofit youth volunteer organization, Kids Korps USA. Our organization's mission is to instill in America's youth (ages five to 18) the spirit of giving while providing valuable education in leadership and responsibility. In this position, I write grants, establish collaborative partnerships with community partners, conduct research, develop educational materials, and present papers at conferences. During a panel discussion on youth violence at the Hearst Corporation Auditorium in New York City, facing reporters and cameras, I felt very proud to be an anthropologist. **In the flash of a moment, I knew that I, like other anthropologists, can reach into a toolbox of knowledge and skills to address issues that are so relevant to the future of our children and our nation.** Ours is a journey of discovery; where we are today is a stepping-stone to new forms of knowledge, self-expression, and community service.

Originally appeared in Anthropology Newsletter, *January 1996*
Revised, spring 1998 and fall 1999

Engaging Anthropology in the Nonprofit Sector

Karin E. Tice
Formative Evaluation Research Associates

Anthropologists have a special role to play in weaving a new global social fabric, in which diversity is valued and can flourish. This would be a world where cross-cultural communication and collaboration facilitate innovative solutions to social problems, and improved processes and systems exist to mediate conflicts when they arise. I have had the great **privilege of working with people of vision** who value what I have to contribute as an anthropologist to the initiatives, structures, processes, and programs they are developing and implementing.

My grandmother, mother, and father began my informal training as an anthropologist. My grandmother was fascinated by the world and its people, was an educator and a world traveler, and was always asking questions. My mother is an artist and an educator and has spent her career reweaving social fabrics wherever and in whatever ways she can. Her work has brought the generations together in schools, has reached gang girls in inner-city Chicago, and has involved business school students in community service with at-risk middle school students. The materials she has developed have been disseminated worldwide. Both women deeply valued service and taught me that I have a responsibility to make the world a little better. My father, a philosopher of education, encouraged the academic and conceptual side of my learning.

My formal education in anthropology began at Friends World College, where we were challenged to focus on major social problems as the core of our curriculum and to work with grassroots organizations around the world addressing those concerns in innovative ways. I received my M.A. and Ph.D. in anthropology from the Joint Program in Applied Anthropology and Education at Teachers College and Columbia University in 1989. **I studied the history of applied anthropology—the good, the bad, and the ugly**—and learned that engaging in applied research requires one to ask difficult questions. My early research focused on the globalization of craft production and its implications for indigenous women.

Serendipity took a hand in my career. Still writing my dissertation, I moved back to Ann Arbor, my home community, and looked for part-time work. Through a friend I was asked to do some interviewing for Formative Evaluation Research Associates (FERA) part-time for about two weeks. **Fourteen years, a book, and two children later I am still with FERA** and am now a partner along with John Seeley, FERA's founder. FERA is celebrating its 25th anniversary this year! We have been a virtual company for the past seven years—meaning our entire staff of about 20 works from home. FERA is dedicated to enhancing the performance of nonprofit organizations committed to improving the quality of life for any person. This occurs through conducting formative evaluations, facilitating strategic planning efforts, and teaching about evaluation. **We work with local, national, and international nonprofit organizations.**

I identify myself at FERA and with my clients as an anthropologist. Sometimes I get a blank or quizzical look, but increasingly clients value what anthropologists have to contribute. They are searching for someone to help them delve into the complexities of multisite, multilevel, collaborative efforts and to figure out whether they are making a difference and, if so, for whom and in what ways. They value the holistic perspective anthropology offers and its methodologies, which are capable of handling complex, interrelated, and constantly changing situations.

I have worked with a wide range of clients in the past, including organizations as diverse as the American Association of Higher Education, the Ford Foundation, the Alabama Institute for the Deaf and Blind, and the American Library Association. My current work focuses primarily on community foundations and on youth development. Since 1991, I have been documenting and evaluating the Michigan Community Foundations' Youth Project (MCFYP), designed to stimulate community foundation growth and to involve youth in philanthropy, service, and leadership roles in their communities. I work closely with the Council of Michigan Foundations to evaluate a cluster of grants related to MCFYP. For example, community foundations throughout Michigan have created 96 Youth Advisory Councils comprising youth ages 12–18. These youth conduct needs and asset assessments, serve as grant makers, engage in fund-raising with foundation board members, and stimulate youth volunteerism in their communities. I have worked with adult and youth stakeholders to develop evaluation questions and success indicators. Some of the evaluation activities that followed from these questions are (1) snapshots of Youth Advisory Councils statewide taken at different points in time, (2) case studies of five community foundations and their Youth Advisory Councils, (3) a longitudinal study of youth which includes case studies of a sample of youth, (4) development of best practices, and (5) a monograph that has been widely disseminated.

My anthropological training has been highly useful in several ways. First, I draw from anthropological theories to understand the underlying assumptions individuals and organizations make about social change. Second, I spend a great deal of my time "in the field." I use my past experiences with how to gain entry and what questions to ask and my knowledge about some of the potential benefits and drawbacks to being an outsider or to working in my own backyard.

As an applied anthropologist I work with stakeholder groups to design evaluations, to interpret data, and to develop lessons learned and recommendations for the future. I implement evaluations using a wide range of methodologies, including participant-observation, interviews, surveys, instrumented group interviews (like focus groups), mapping, and site visits. The research findings are presented in a variety of ways and settings, including oral presentations, written reports, data summaries, and monographs. I also teach clients and stakeholders about evaluation. As a FERA partner, I am also responsible for marketing and running the company.

FERA underscores the value of participatory, utilization-focused evaluations, an approach that aligns with my philosophy. Increasingly, I am working with foundations and capacity-building organizations to build new local, regional, and statewide infrastructures for grassroots participation in community problem solving and resource distribution. **My advice to anthropologists entering the applied field is to think about how you want to make a difference, find people who have similar concerns, and create an opportunity for yourself.**

Originally appeared in Anthropology Newsletter, *March 1993*
Revised, spring 1998 and summer 1999

The Business of a Sustainable Career: Environmental Anthropology

P. J. Puntenney
Environmental and Human Systems Management

Tam Ormiston, Kim In-Hwan, and P. J. Puntenney, Seoul National University, 1993

It is exciting work to be a part of the next generation of anthropologists contributing to what is becoming known as "environmental anthropology." Essentially I wear two hats, first as founder and executive director of Environmental and Human Systems Management (E&HSM). Second, whenever my time allows, I am an adjunct research scientist affiliated with the University of Michigan. E&HSM is a consulting firm created to assist organizations, nationally and internationally, in managing environmental issues. Working with senior management on needs identification and problem solving, E&HSM provides services that include planning, evaluation, research, communications, and training. Over the years I have found that **my role has evolved from that of a technical consultant to one of adviser helping clients to shape policy-making strategies.**

Much of the work carried out in the environmental arena has been focused on environmental services, technology, regulations, the hard sciences, and the research and application of these knowledge bases. Yet there is a growing realization that more expertise is needed in interpreting the dynamic interactions between human and natural systems. **My work focuses on the human dimensions of environmental issues.** Clients are generally decision makers who shape policy and decide the direction of future program initiatives. In moving through the stages of problem solving with them, the challenge is to put into place an ongoing learning process. This transformation from an unorganized base of knowledge to decision making "within a context" about actions, choices, and interventions is usually shaped by ethical and moral considerations, bureaucratic and organizational constraints, external and internal organizational relationships, and differing doses of good luck and misfortune.

The nature of this kind of work is such that it is **imperative for me to be current in several related disciplines.** The decision makers I work with feel it is important to be informed from multiple sources of data that span technical, political, economic, ecological, and social/cultural factors. Environmental knowledge is in a constant state of flux—a reflection of not only the complexity but also the amount of information being developed on environmental and human systems interrelationships. Knowing this, I have maintained an academic appointment through which I have close contact with my colleagues in the field and especially with students.

Frequently, decision makers are asking questions that are anthropological in nature, but the anthropological perspective has been lacking, not to mention the anthropologist. For me, the **American Anthropological Association annual meetings have provided an effective vehicle for creating a forum to bring knowledgeable professionals from other disciplines together with anthropologists.** Just such a forum on culture and the environment from the 1989 meetings in Washington, D.C., has led to further involvement of anthropologists with leaders from the environmental arena in shaping an international agenda for community-based conservation. It also led to the creation of jobs specifically for anthropologists within these organizations. Working closely with NAPA Bulletin Series coeditor Pamela Amoss, we took this effort one step further. Authors were selected from the session to write about these issues and the emerging models from their work. This resulted in NAPA Bulletin 15, entitled "Global Ecosystems: Creating Options through Anthropological Perspectives" (1995). At the 1995 meetings in Washington, D.C., Leslie Sponsel, Lenora Bohren, and I organized a similar session to shed light on another dimension of environmental anthropology: *cultural and biological diversity.* Again we involved professionals outside of anthropology, providing a forum to discuss key ideas and issues with the anthropological community.

The foundation for the way I approach my work was laid early in my graduate career by three anthropologists, **Lucien and Jane Hanks and Shepard Forman, who supported and encouraged my intellectual inquiries into the discipline as a bridge to the other sciences addressing environmental concerns.** This, plus the intellectual discipline of working in an interdisciplinary climate at graduate school, has served me well. At the time, I worked with faculty in natural resources, engineering, public health, anthropology, psychology, education, urban planning, and urban technological environmental planning (a unique university-wide Ph.D. program within the University of Michigan). I learned to communicate with diverse audiences, to work in interdisciplinary team settings, to understand the dynamic relationship between good theory and the application of anthropological knowledge, and to appreciate the illusive art of writing. Having decided to pursue a joint doctorate, I also learned more than I ever wanted to know about the intricate politics within the university community.

Like many people in this country, I had heard of Margaret Mead, and early on in my graduate career, I became familiar with her work—"Be Aware of the Ghost of Mead." **What I had not anticipated was the profound influence she would continually have on my career.** At each major juncture in my career I have observed that colleagues who have been influential in shaping our thinking about the public engagement of anthropology and in turn have influenced my own work either studied directly under Mead, went to school with her, were her colleagues, and/or served on policy-making committees/task forces with her. The reach and influence of this great anthropologist on professionals active in the application of anthropological knowledge, I believe, has been and continues to be extraordinary.

In 1983, however, the year I graduated, this was not at all clear. Prior to entering a year's fieldwork in 1979, I had been offered five different positions in Washington, D.C., to head up international environmental efforts with full salary while I worked on my research. I chose to stay fully emerged in academia. At the time, I thought I would have job security upon finishing. Then along came the change of the presidential administration. Upon returning from the field, I found that my job security had vanished along with governmental support for many environmental programs. **It was a sobering moment to realize how closely my environmental career choice was connected to the ups and downs of the national political arena.** Marketing my newly acquired intellectual achievements was never discussed in graduate school, let alone the job market realities that I now faced.

I found in the pursuit of career activities that it was easy once outside the academic environment to lose one's professional identity. There was no academic community with a dean, department chair, mentor, friends, or colleagues reminding me daily of my identity, professional expectations, and where I was headed—graduation, right? Before finishing my degree, I had written a research grant that was funded to conduct postgraduate work. During this period of time, I picked up the odd consultancy and watched the job opportunities continue to dwindle as the grant came to an end. I had reached a point at which it became apparent that I needed to formally establish my consulting firm. About this time, an anthropologist friend returned to Ann Arbor, having finished most of her graduate work at Columbia. We talked about our work, and she introduced me to the associations where I was soon to find many colleagues. Within these organizations, I discovered that the small minority of people working on the "people" problem side of environmental issues was not so small after all. **As I was not academically based, a number one priority for me was to figure out how to stay professionally connected and to build my own support community.** Within the Society for Applied Anthropology, the Washington Association of Professional Anthropologists, NAPA, and the High Plains Society for Applied Anthropology, I found those linkages.

As my field and academic experiences accumulated over the years, I have moved from a bewildered graduate to serving as a senior foreign policy adviser to the Ministry of Environment in Korea, helping to facilitate the Northeast Asia Environmental Cooperation Network, and serving in a senior advisory capacity to several countries in Asia, Latin America, Africa, Europe, and North America on environmental matters. Other clients have included such organizations as Ford Motor Company, the World Wildlife Fund, the U.S. Forest Service, the U.S. National Park Service, the World Bank, the World Conservation Union, and my own local community. One of my more interesting projects recently has been to serve as advisory to the film *Right to Hope,* which links culture, art, and the global environment as part of the 1995 celebration of the United Nations' 50th anniversary. It is hard to say what will unfold for me in the next five years, but the very nature of the expanding environmental arena would seem to insure that environmental anthropology will hold a central role.

Notes from the Field: Postscript, 1995 to the Present

Currently, my work involves initiatives with the U.N. Council on Sustainable Development Post-Rio meetings in New York and serving as a delegate of the U.N. Environment and Development–United Kingdom. Again, **Mead's influence is felt in multiple ways at the United Nations.** During the meetings it is not unusual for her name to come up as the standard-bearer of excellence. Today, distinguished colleagues such as Darrell Posey embody Mead's public legacy. His work on integrating "indigenous peoples" into the policy and planning structure of the World Conservation Union, and the impact of his creation of a global professional network via the Internet has placed "indigenous peoples" within the mainstream of U.N. work. This is good news for anthropology and anthropologists but leaves many unanswered questions and certainly uncharted waters.

As for myself, I am **continuously challenged to articulate to policy makers the important role of the human dimensions of global environmental issues,** especially those topics we so easily talk about among our colleagues, for example, cultural systems, equity, indigenous peoples, rights, interrelationships, holistic perspectives, youth, women, and knowledge systems. The voice from the nongovernmental organization community is new and is reshaping the U.N. system to include the thinking from civil society (ordinary people) in its policy deliberations. **The actual mechanisms to channel the Other into the U.N. system are being recreated, leaving many of us caught between the old traditions set down in 1948 along the lines of the old European nation-states and the pressing needs of the 21st century for democratic participation in governance.**

An outgrowth of my work to link anthropological knowledge with diverse professional audiences has evolved into two forthcoming books, *The Knowledge to Act: Coming to Terms with Environmental and Human Rights* (University of Iowa Press) and *A Lasting Impression: Interpreting the Human Dimensions of Global Environmental Issues.* Keeping up with the continuing need for professional development, I will be taking advantage of Harvard Law School's portfolio of seminars for senior management, "The Executive as Negotiator." Although I was not aware of it until the business world invented the term, my firm is what is currently called a "life-style business," and I am an entrepreneur. This is important to note be-cause **the social sciences are not at all like the hard sciences, or business, or law, or medicine, whereby, outside the academy, there are definite market niches, salary charts, and career benchmarks.** And if we opt for a nontraditional professional track, we need to know something about the skills needed in those areas and more.

On a final note, the challenge in the near future for environmental an-thropology, and in particular for my own professional endeavors, is the ar-ticulation of our essential role on this world stage. The environmental arena essentially operates within the confines of value-based alternatives. Inter-estingly, from the Eastern and Western spiritual traditions, strong sources of leadership are emerging and are transforming local and international policy-making venues. For example, the prominent Buddhist leader, His Holiness the Dalai Lama, and the Anglican Bishop, Desmond Tutu, have through their own actions brought global attention to interdependence, ethics, and the necessity of global dialogues. **This intersection between environment, policy making, ethics, and spiritual traditions is a fertile ground for anthropology.**

Originally appeared in Anthropology Newsletter, *November 1995*
Revised, spring 1998 and summer 1999

Practicing Anthropology in the Human Rights Arena

Barbara Rose Johnston
Center for Political Ecology

Barbara Johnston

Acknowledging the "human rights" theme of the 1994 American Anthropological Association (AAA) meeting, NAPA column editor Paula Sabloff asked me to write a contribution for this work. I was to describe how practicing anthropologists influence people's thinking about human rights and play a significant role in human rights intervention cases. I cannot do justice to this topic. Forensic anthropologists, historical archaeologists, medical anthropologists, environmental anthropologists, development anthropologists—colleagues with all sorts of disciplinary interests—are immersed in human rights–related struggles and continue to struggle with human problems, arguing for basic rights, fighting the battles, and occasionally winning. Confronting the task of summing it up or focusing on the efforts of others is too big a task, given the constraints of time and space.

What I would like to do here is comment on factors that inhibit our ability as a discipline to have an effect in the human rights arena and point out some areas where focusing our efforts may have positive results. My comments are derived from an assessment of my own experiences (with limited success and marked failures) to practice anthropology in the international environmental policy and human rights arenas. Between 1991 and 1997 I served as **organizer and coordinator of a group of international and interdisciplinary scholars whose aim was to document the sociocultural dimensions of environmental crisis in support of a United Nations study on "human rights and the environment."** We produced and broadly distributed a series of reports, public policy documents, letters, and formal publications. The primary objectives of this project were to broaden the notion of what constitutes human rights abuse, to demonstrate that groups as well as individuals experience human rights abuse, and to analyze the conditions and contexts that produce, legitimize, and reproduce victimization. Our aim was to insert the anthropological voice in environmental policy arenas and conversely emphasize the roles that environmental conditions and context play in human rights abuse. We have had some success in that these ideas are reflected in the current language of the "Draft Declaration on Human Rights and the Environment" (adopted by the Sub-Commission on the Prevention of Discrimination and Protection of Minorities and being considered for adoption by the U.N. Commission on Human Rights). And our material has been published in the "environmental media." (See, for example, *Who Pays the Price? The Sociocultural Context of Environmental Crisis,* released in August 1994. This book was the first social science book published by Island Press, a nonprofit environmental policy publisher.) On the other hand, success is hard to gauge, as the gap between language and action seems almost unbridgeable.

Comments here are also significantly influenced by conversations and debates at the Atlanta AAA "human rights" meeting in 1996, where many colleagues enthusiastically embraced the human rights mission of anthropology. Others expressed surprise at the apparent disciplinary acceptance and approval of a "human rights" focus (in light of the past struggles to achieve some semblance of disciplinary respectability). And still others expressed dismay at the **threats posed by the overtly political nature of human rights work, which threatens (as one person voiced in one of my sessions) to "erode the nature, meaning, and scientific objectivity of our discipline."**

The debated and very heated arguments over ideology, authoritative voice, relativism, and ethics—over the essential meaning and appropriate use of anthropology—mirror broader conflicts in our academic and political institutions. These issues are not new; they will always be with us as they are with other actors in society. What is our responsibility to society and to humanity? Whom do we speak for? What facet or version of reality prompts us to act? What are the implications of our actions? How do we accept responsibility for those implications?

In many ways, **the struggle to protect basic human rights represents the ideological heart and soul of our discipline.** We seek to define and understand humanity. Our intellectual pursuits involve us (in varying degrees) with humanity. Our involvement inevitably requires confronting the ugly and, some would say, evil sides of humanity. Involvement and confrontation inextricably link us to the experience, and, thus, we struggle to protect basic human rights because we see it as our moral and ethical responsibility.

Many of us are attracted to anthropology because we are challenged by the potential force of its human focus—or because the burden of maintaining a sense of self and self-worth in an ever changing world is eased by a sense of direction, shared identity, and common purpose. Or perhaps we simply find anthropology an effective means to scratch personal intellectual itches. As with every human endeavor, there are selfless and selfish sides to our action. All of us, at one time or another, struggle with the contradictory ways in which our desire to *do* something inhibits our ability to comfortably sustain our lives (income, relationships, careers, life). Failure to recognize the influences of our personal interests and to resolve the conflicts created by our personal contradictions is perhaps the central inhibiting factor in the ability of anthropologists and anthropology to *act* in an effective manner.

There are significant barriers to recognizing and dealing with this ideological contradiction. Our culture (i.e., Western culture, the culture of science, the culture of our discipline) exists in fragmented spaces and places in the mind, spirit, and material world. This fragmentation reinforces our tendency to frame problems in tightly defined, bounded terms that suggest logical and linear solutions—strategies and methods used to achieve scientific "objectivity" (and presumably a verifiable version of "truth").

Conscious use of "objectivity" has its place, but exclusionary use of objectivity has its dangers. The pursuit of objectivity hinges on our ability to practice the fine art of distancing: distancing ourselves from reality to the point that we can observe, isolate, and distill facets of the human experience without losing our grasp of reality—hovering in the air while still managing to keep our feet on the ground. Forcing the complex nature of human crisis into a scientific framework implies a series of compromises. Both the act of distancing and the fragmentation of complex reality into discrete analytical units carry analytical risks and deny the true nature of humanity, human experience, human problems, and human needs. Reality is messy, complex, and organically entrenched. Furthermore, and germane to a discussion of human rights, the distance required in the pursuit of objectivity threatens to compromise both our commitment and our ability to act.

How we define problems, focus our lives' energies, conduct our work, and articulate our findings influences our role as actors in society. For me, there is a huge difference between an anthropology that seeks to understand humanity and an anthropology that embraces humanity. One defines problems and seeks answers at an arm's distance, avoiding risk and the uncomfortable confrontation with the implications of action. The other is consciously grounded and inextricably linked to the diverse and often painful realities to human existence. Most of us frame our problems and design our research and activism somewhere in the middle ground, forced by the reality of our self-interest to limit and compromise idealistic action.

Much of the social science attention to human rights abuse focuses on defining the nature of problems in a descriptive and analytical fashion with the twin goals of understanding the production and reproduction of human rights abuses and working toward formal acknowledgments of culpability. This is certainly true of my work with the U.N. Commission on Human Rights Sub-Commission on the Prevention of Discrimination and Protection of Minorities study on "human rights and the environment." Focusing our efforts on influencing the thought and language of international human rights policy seemed an important yet relatively comfortable way of handling our responsibility to the communities we studied. **We whispered in the ears of a few policy makers rather than shouting our protest on the ground in concert with members of our "communities."** This strategy was consciously employed. Our global analysis was structured with an audience of international policy makers in mind and with the objective of influencing institutions of power and authority—studying and acting "up." Two years into the endeavor, after analyzing the efficacy of our efforts (or relative lack thereof), I diversified our policy "targets" and research objectives by (1) emphasizing interdisciplinary feedback mechanisms (for example, creating a human environmental rights network with the goal of stimulating research) and (2) broadening our "policy-maker" audience by obtaining funds to freely distribute our work among national and international politicians and governments as well as various human rights and environmental organizations.

The "human rights and environment" project, like many efforts to apply anthropology, demonstrates our analytical strength and praxis weakness. We are very good at identifying problems and causal factors. For a number of reasons, we are not very good at suggesting ways to solve problems. When we do recommend strategies to resolve problems, our recommendations are often ineffectively articulated, voiced in the wrong circles, or simply ignored. **Our role of adviser rarely carries political authority.**

What can we do? Some have suggested we need to encourage more anthropologists to carve out careers in policy arenas, to seek out positions with real authority. **Others suggest restructuring training programs and *retraining programs to provide ourselves with the knowledge and tools to effectively work within political institutions.*** These are needed changes, changes currently under way. These and other actions, much more than idealistic statements and rhetoric, will determine whether we can rise to the continual need to "reinvent" anthropology.

Today's crises require a recognition that answers are diverse. No single notion, model, or approach is sufficiently capable to handle problems that are synergistic and cumulative. To the colleague who voiced his dismay at the political path that human rights work takes us on, I say all sorts of paths are necessary and all sorts of risks must be taken. We need the continuum of actors and actions within our discipline, and that continuum includes those who *do* as well as those who distance themselves from action.

To conclude these brief observations, I believe our discipline has the potential to play a hugely significant role in the human rights arena. Our analytical capabilities, holistic perspective, and intensive experience with all levels of the sociopolitical web provide us with the tools to make some sense out of chaos. We have the ability to identify and seize significant threads; unravel the tangled complexity of history, culture, political economy, and environmental contact; and, thus, identify where action might be most effective in resolving problems and preventing conflict. But, for our efforts to be noticed, we must find ways of understanding the nature of power and assert ourselves more aggressively into the system of power.

Our disciplinary approach to human rights (meaning that of the collective community of anthropologists in professional organizations, academic departments, and various private and governmental institutions) focuses almost exclusively on understanding the origins and evolution of human rights problems. Relatively little attention is paid to "postcrisis" periods. There is a need to broaden our research and praxis and seriously consider the patterns, efficacy, and implications of response—what people, organizations, and institutions propose and do in response to human rights violations. We need to identify the ideological assumptions structuring responses and consider the sociopolitical implications of those responses. This attention must be critical (pointing out inhibiting factors) as well as visionary (documenting cases of successful resolution and isolating those mechanisms that proved crucial in redistributing power and in sharing the consequences). And, finally, we must acknowledge that the efficacy of our efforts hinges on our ability to communicate our findings in diverse ways and in multiple arenas. What is the point of studying humanity if our sole audience is ourselves?

Coda

In rereading my December 1994 NAPA profile on human rights, I find little I would change. This essay explores anthropological praxis and argues for a **stronger, more aggressive effort to assert anthropology in human policy and planning-solving processes.** I argue for scholarship as the means to effect change—to understand, shape, and (ideally) transform the degenerative aspects of our condition.

While this essay details what it is I believe and attempt with my anthropology, I have not provided a profile of how I sustain and assert this work. Briefly, the human rights and environment project represented an effort to assert the human rights voice in environmental policy realms at the local, national, and international levels and, conversely, to assert an environmental perspective in the human rights arena. This work was initially sponsored by the Society for Applied Anthropology (SfAA), which endorsed the formation of a committee, reviewed and endorsed our reports, and co-sponsored a grant from the Nathan Cummings Foundation to disseminate our findings in broad political settings. This work has also been supported by the Center for Political Ecology in Santa Cruz, California, where I am the senior research fellow.

Currently, my research and advocacy efforts are stimulated by issues relating to my membership on the AAA Committee for Human Rights and sustained by periodic lectureships at the University of California at Santa Cruz, as well as consulting work as director of the environmental anthropology project for the SfAA (a project funded through a five-year cooperative agreement with the U.S. Environmental Protection Agency). This last commitment involves a broad range of administrative, research, and praxis work and is perhaps best described as an effort to assert social science into U.S. community-based environmental planning and problem-solving processes.

I believe that **the most powerful anthropology is that which is problem focused, shaped in collaborative ways, and projected in interdisciplinary and broader public realms.** I do community-based work, where the "field" is my own backyard. I came of age professionally in the Virgin Island community I chose to call home. For ten years, St. Thomas was the center of my world—an island floating alone in the sea, and all the world's events were interpreted in relation to that rock. As I began to see the global networks of relations, boundaries became fluid, and my notion of community-based work expanded to include a collection of communities linked across time and space, defined by varied conditions, events, and experiences. If there is a common thread to my experiences, it is the fascination with, and periodic immersions within, systems of power. I am interested in the genesis and structure of crisis, in the range of responses, and in the possibility of radical transformation. However, as I continue to explore the fluidity of power, the tension between local and global contexts, and the structure and mechanisms employed to shape or redirect the loci of power, I tread softly. I am keenly aware that documenting the relationship between human misery, degenerative conditions, and the range of subsequent responses produces information that can be manipulated. Engaged, problem-focused anthropology of "trouble" is a double-edged sword—it holds great promise yet provokes great fear. Studying the impact of problem-solving responses has the potential to produce conceptual recipes for stimulating further social chaos, for mitigating or resolving crises, or, perhaps, for stifling that which seriously threatens the status quo.

Originally appeared in Anthropology Newsletter, *February 1995*
"Coda" text added, spring 1998
Revised, summer 1999

Working as an Independent Consultant

Linda A. Camino
Camino and Associates

Linda Camino

As an independent consultant, I am a professional researcher and adviser. My clients include governmental agencies, private foundations, and nonprofit national and local organizations. One of my concentrations is evaluation research, a special brand of policy research. Put simply, evaluation attempts to identify and assess the strengths, limitations, and best practices of an initiative, institution, program, or project; locate the contexts under which these practices occur; and infuse the record with new ideas, ideally so that improvements and new policies can be made.

Evaluation offers a good niche to the ethnographic researcher. The very fact that evaluation can be a required or accepted component of program operation provides an edge for the would-be evaluator. The client needs the services of a trained researcher—typically at the Ph.D. level. More and more, **as stakeholders recognize the importance that context holds to revealing "what works and what doesn't," ethnography is catching hold as an integral methodology and conceptual framework.** Anthropologists, however, are not the only ones to occupy this niche. There is a host of professional researchers in many disciplines who now specialize in ethnography.

What added value can an anthropologist bring to the needs and concerns of clients who wish to engage ethnographers? In my consulting practice, I use my knowledge and experience as an anthropological ethnographer, both explicitly and implicitly, to shape and guide the work. **To articulate the anthropological difference, I draw on two sides of ethnography: the technical and the imaginative.**

With respect to the technical, I discuss in early client negotiations how I, as an anthropologist, and how the ethnographic method can address common initial questions about the evaluation approach and research design. Client questions usually include, "How can we reconcile partner agency needs with the funder's needs? What indicators should be used? What is the appropriate design, and what methods should be employed? How can we best demonstrate impact? When is evaluation best done, and how long does it take? We've had bad experiences with evaluators in the past—how can the evaluation be as participatory as possible?" We also discuss the skills needed to carry out good ethnographic research—interviewing, listening, observation, instrument construction, literature and document review, analysis, synthesis, interpretation, and writing and presentation—as well as the special ways anthropologists use these.

I am not merely a technician, however. In most cases, I have found it a myth of hokum that, outside of academe, I am hired and valued solely for my technical skills. **There are intellectual, moral, and even spiritual dimensions that permeate my work.** They derive from ethnographic experience and anthropological training, yet they are not "skills" in a mechanistic sense. They are, rather, those **qualities that make up what I call the anthropological ethnographic imagination.** What are some forms this imagination takes?

First, anthropological training has honed my ability to examine and think about things holistically. Holistic thinking means I am in a position to see many aspects of the same phenomenon and to locate the situated views of different stakeholders. It also entails an ability to see beyond short-term, "fix-it" solutions to deeper causes and broader effects. My clients spend much of their time looking at and dealing with the trees in their own corner of the forest. Often, what they are seeking to learn more about is the forest itself—its contour, composition, and texture. For the evaluator, a holistic view assumes critical importance because one needs to help stakeholders think reflexively about their philosophies, policies, assumptions, and operations in order to stimulate them to close (or at least recognize) the gap between what they think they are doing and what they are actually doing.

Second, as an anthropologist, I know about collaboration and social networks. **We practicing anthropologists write a lot about how, in the world outside of academe, we are expected to work as team players.** The implication is that collaboration is not a typical feature of anthropological training. This was not my experience, however. My doctoral fieldwork imparted well the lessons of collaboration. (Regrettably, subsequent academic socialization and its ethos of individualism often encourage us to "unlearn" or "forget" aspects of interdependence in work once we return from the field.) Not only did my fieldwork necessitate that I get out there and scrub around in a particular culture; it also demanded that I work collaboratively. My hosts had lives to lead. They did not greet me with hosannas simply because I was there to "study them." As such, I found that **reciprocity and cooperation were necessary to establish trusting relationships and gain access to their thoughts, theories, hopes, dreams, activities, and artifacts—in short, their lives.** And I learned that ethnography is not "collecting" data but is, instead, a dialectical process, as understanding is built up through dynamic interactions with informants.

Evaluation clients often operate in a world of shifting, if not shrinking, funds and resources, and they want to know, or are required to consider, how to partner and collaborate more effectively in order to leverage resources so that maximum program benefit might be attained. The fact that I have had direct, extended field experience in knowing how to approach and work with a variety of players, as well as have secondhand knowledge gained through anthropological ethnographies regarding how groups of people tend to organize social networks and operate through the connections, bestows enormous advantages.

No less important in my work are dimensions of the anthropological imagination, which can be called "spiritual." Certainly, the ethnographic enterprise uses systematic epistemologies and methods that must be logically and empirically demonstrated. But what anthropologist (indeed, what scientist) has not admitted at some time that enthusiasm for the work has been fueled by moments of sudden intuitive understanding? And what anthropologist has not been compelled at some time by a caring motivation for the people he or she works with?

Frequently, of course, one cannot discuss the "spiritual" aspects directly with clients (at least not at the outset), lest one be dismissed as somewhat "kooky." After all, one is there as a researcher, and clients have certain images and expectations about research. Nonetheless, clients appreciate willingness to establish personal relationships and a humanistic approach based on intuitive insights.

For my work as an anthropological evaluator, this orientation has many ramifications. Evaluation is as much a psychological concept as anything. It is hedged with much anxiety. Because evaluation is also situated in relationships of power, the anxiety is typically reality based. Accordingly, I have found that evaluation, similar to anthropological fieldwork, obliges more than a detached, objective stance. Many nonprofit practitioners delivering services and administering human services programs are committed to their work, and they expect me and my research endeavors to be infused with similar regard. Besides, **caring and intuition go a long way toward creating environments in which stakeholders feel respected and comfortable.** Such a climate inclines various individuals to contribute positively to evaluation activities, as well as to use the results.

Research and practice represent different paradigms. Research emphasizes the "study of," while practice concerns the integration of knowledge with social, political, economic, and cultural dynamics that ultimately affect action. **Practical ethnography straddles both these paradigms.** Anthropologist practitioners need to master action-oriented competencies and roles in addition to those oriented toward the discovery of knowledge. As a consultant, I wear many hats: researcher, documenter, analyst, evaluator, writer, information broker, teacher, facilitator, coach, counselor, confidant, leader, and follower. To be sure, the technical side of ethnography enables me to carry out these roles. But technology is not enough.

I got my degree from the University of Virginia, concentrating in symbolic and medical anthropology. I also held an internship at the university's medical school, working with a diverse array of physicians, clinicians, and patients. Certainly, the confluence of skills, intellect, ethics, and spirit that have found their way into my practice germinated in my training with these individuals. They were also incubated in 18 months of fieldwork. Moreover, I didn't stop using the ethnographic imagination once I earned my degree and began working outside of academe. This is not to say that the ethnographic imagination is easy to continually exercise in the world of praxis. It is, however, worthwhile. With modesty, I take satisfaction that, far more often than not, the results of my research and advice are used to good effect by stakeholders. I have been told by clients that they appreciate my services because I portray their programs and endeavors with vividness and sensitivity, identify the "real" concerns of various stakeholder groups, challenge their thinking, and formulate helpful recommendations. **It is the combination of anthropological and ethnographic skills and imagination, mediated through the particular ways I configure the applications, that constitutes the added value I can bring to clients.**

Note

Many of the thoughts I touch on here are elaborated in my 1997 article, "What Can Anthropologists Offer Ethnographic Program Evaluation?" (in *Practicing Anthropology in a Postmodern World: Lessons and Insights from Federal Contract Research,* edited by Michael C. Reed, pp. 41–57, NAPA Bulletin, 17 [Arlington, VA: American Anthropological Association]).

Originally appeared in Anthropology Newsletter, *September 1996*
Revised, spring 1998 and summer 1999

Projects Parse My Work Life

Edward Liebow
Environmental Health and Social Policy Center

I started the Environmental Health and Social Policy Center in 1997 as an organization for policy research, program evaluation, and social science training for policy makers. This was after working about 11 years for the Battelle Memorial Institute. Working at Battelle was, for me, a formative experience, but I eventually came to feel that its organizational structure created an unproductive division between social science research and technology applications. **I became especially interested in creating a new organizational form, one that does not assume the need for a "technology fix" but, rather, aims to promote a broad public understanding of the social causes and consequences of environmental hazards.**

"Projects" parse my work life at the center: They frame data collection, analysis, and reporting; they create and organize relations with colleagues and collaborating outfits; and they provide the excuse and the means for building new research tools and skills. **The center's projects all deal with energy, environmental, and community development issues and almost always aim to resolve conflicts over the protection of local rights and resources.**

I am involved in an ongoing social demography project to determine whether Indian people living near the Hanford nuclear works in the Pacific Northwest may have received higher doses of radiation than their non-Indian counterparts, especially in the years at the end of World War II. This work is sponsored by the U.S. Centers for Disease Control and Prevention and is distinguished (thanks to staunch advocacy by several tribal representatives and by University of Colorado anthropologist Deward Walker) by the tribes' unprecedented degree of control over how their members' experiences are to be represented. I continue my involvement with the **U.S. Department of Energy in its efforts to place its dealings with Indian tribes on a "government-to-government" basis, rather than going through intermediaries like the Bureau of Indian Affairs or other governmental agencies.** I am involved in some strategic planning work for the energy, defense, and health and human services departments to determine what organizational changes they face in complying with the Clinton administration's environmental justice initiatives.

The Environmental Health and Social Policy Center is a private organization, and I am its sole owner. **I initially considered incorporating as a not-for-profit outfit, but after much soul-searching I decided not to.** The not-for-profit status would communicate a certain neutrality (educational activities are permitted but not lobbying and other advocacy efforts). **The not-for-profit status deflects suspicions about the motives for fund-raising activities and is, at least in concept, accountable to a community through the appointment of a board of directors. It is this accountability and the board of directors, however, that have been problematic for me.** I have served on several boards, and I have watched my wife, who is also a professional anthropologist, work throughout her entire postgraduate career in the not-for-profit sector. Our collective experiences have taught us that **it takes special attributes and skills to be a productive board member.** Unfortunately, in our experience, it has too often been the case that working with a board of directors, as required by law to retain a preferred tax status, redirects attention and resources to board development—that is, to building the board members' skills to the point at which they can productively serve the mission of the organization.

Just as I aim to have the center avoid reproducing the formal schism between social science and technology, I have also set out to **avoid recreating the built-in tension between staff and board that characterizes so many nonprofit organizations.** I *do* believe in community accountability for my organization's work, however. As the center enters its third year, we are experimenting with an approach that combines project hires, internships for community members, and a community-based steering committee (whose members' compensation is budgeted) to review proposal drafts, work plans, data collection and analysis protocols, and the selection of co-facilitators for training projects.

Back in 1986, I was the first cultural anthropologist the Battelle Memorial Institute ever hired. Battelle is a private, not-for-profit technology research and development organization with a staff of about 8,000 scientists and engineers. Most of the staff is located either at the institute's headquarters in Columbus, Ohio, or in Richland, Washington, where it operates a national laboratory for the Department of Energy. The Seattle-based Human Affairs Research Centers, which hired me originally, held by far the largest concentration of Battelle social scientists until it was disbanded in 1996. In 1999, Battelle employed six post–M.A. cultural anthropologists, all working on environmental and health care policy issues.

Throughout my project-based career, what they say about ethnography applied in policy settings has held true: the inquiry is inevitably limited by time and money and by boundaries we place around dimensions of social life in which we permit the government to intervene. **I always work as part of an interdisciplinary team and find my interactions with my colleagues—sociologists, social psychologists, and geographers—to be terrifically sustaining. From my perspective, anthropologists cannot afford not to collaborate with social scientists from other disciplines.** Indeed, we anthropologists normally are trained to be collaborative, and ultimately it undermines our research and our discipline to further promote the image of the ethnographer as lone ranger.

My training attracted attention among the center's sponsors, and I was not shy about declaring there to be a core that sets anthropology apart. For me, this core is packed with an identifiable institutional infrastructure, a massive knowledge base covering the sweep of human history and culture, a methodological repertory that both unites and atomizes us, and a specific ideological orientation to the communities that form the subjects of our work. **I tend to dwell less on what sets us apart, however, and more on what we need to exchange with our cousins in other disciplines and intellectual traditions.** I suppose I derived this emphasis on interdisciplinary work early in my training. As an undergraduate at Carleton College, my studies in anthropology and sociology were combined in a single program. My first graduate research assistantship at Arizona State University, where I completed my M.A. and Ph.D., was not in the Anthropology Department but, rather, across the sidewalk in the Environmental Studies Department. At both schools, the emphasis was heavy on theory and on looking for careful reasoning wherever one could find it, not just in certain journals or sections of the library stacks. In particular, at Carleton, Paul Riesman challenged me to think more carefully and read widely, while Peggy Barlett gently broke the news to me that I couldn't write worth beans. Jim Eder and Don Bahr eventually inherited my incorrigible self at Arizona State and modeled a long-term involvement with a specific locale. Each in his own way set standards of scholarship that students anywhere would be proud to achieve.

I left school for about five years after completing my course work. I was tired of being totally broke and feeling more than a bit removed from current events that I could see from my front steps. This was the late 1970s, and a thousand people a week were pouring into the Phoenix metropolitan area. I went to work for an environmental planning organization where I was committed to finding ways to give voice to the concerns of those who were becoming increasingly marginalized by this explosive growth. I worked on project after project having to do with water rights and urban growth management in the American Southwest, which taught me a good bit about the nuts and bolts of coping with the pressures of rapid urbanization in a fragile desert setting.

I reached a point in this work at which it became apparent to me that I would need to complete my degree to be able to be at all influential in keeping planners and policy makers mindful of social equity considerations as they charted the region's future. At about this time, Miki Crespi (senior anthropologist at the National Park Service) came through Phoenix to visit a mutual friend, and she persuaded me to ride with her out to a national monument for a courtesy call on the superintendent. We talked the whole way about careers in anthropology, and to this day I can recall Miki's advice on that drive: *Even if you never plan to seek a university appointment, your credibility as an anthropologist depends on you completing the most rigorous, theoretically sound dissertation you are capable of producing.*

My return to formal studies after a five-year absence had a level of focus and productivity that clearly resulted from working outside the university. I worked for the next three years on understanding and articulating the developing sense of place so evident among urban Indian residents in metropolitan Phoenix. This tied together a number of themes involving the social landscape of a rapidly urbanizing frontier and reinforced my commitment to a practitioner's career. Just as I was completing the dissertation and a series of projects at the Phoenix Indian Center, an opportunity surfaced to do some consulting work for Battelle in Seattle. The prospect of leaving a familiar place, friends, and well-established social and political connections was offset by the chance to learn more about another controversial regional resource management scene and, indeed, about a national policy perspective.

Since 1986, I have actively worked to maintain my ties to the world of anthropology. I have held a part-time teaching affiliation with the University of Washington Department of Anthropology for several years; I edit a newsletter for the Committee on Anthropology in Environmental Planning; and I have been involved in organizational activities of NAPA and the Society for Applied Anthropology.

I want to return briefly to the notion of "projects" and how they might take the practitioner toward cultural understanding. Although I would never start to build a house from the roof, I believe it is possible, with a solid theoretical foundation and intentional thinking, to build one's understanding of a particular cultural system starting from any number of vantage points. Brian Foster and Steve Seidman, for example, once organized a whole seminar on social networks around the evolution of their understanding of a particular class of problems. They revealed for us that as they caught sight of a problem's complexity, they realized that they had jumped right into the middle of the problem. They then had to go back and teach themselves a calculus for defining this problem before moving ahead to try and solve it. **The practitioner needs to become especially adept at recognizing vantage points opportunistically and to appreciate that although any single project may afford but a limited glimpse of local insights and experiences, eventually, a series of projects can accumulate into something of less limited benefit.** In my case, specific work may be prompted by an immediate community event or the threat of some outside environmental burden looming. I am convinced, however, that by staying put and acting responsibly on one's formal training, important understandings can develop and be shared to the ultimate benefit of the community that produces them.

Originally appeared in Anthropology Newsletter, *May 1994*
Revised, spring 1998 and summer 1999

Anthropology in the Contemporary Museum

Jonathan Haas
Field Museum

My entrée into museum anthropology came when I was an undergraduate anthropology major at the University of Arizona. I wandered into the Anthropology Department office as a sophomore and asked if there were any jobs available. They sent me over to the contract archaeology program in the Arizona State Museum (ASM), which happened to be excavating a **large Hohokam site** in downtown Phoenix. By chance they were looking for someone to wash potsherds and other artifacts from the site. I then spent **18 months washing more than one million sherds.** This job set a new standard of perfection for the term *boring*. Anyway, by the time I had washed the collection I knew the material better than anyone else, so they had me analyze the same million-plus sherds. Shortly after that, I was hired on my first excavation through the ASM and then took a **full-time position as a staff archaeologist working for the Highway Salvage Program.** The next year, 1972, I moved up to Flagstaff and took a similar staff archaeologist position at the Museum of Northern Arizona before going off to graduate school at Columbia. At Columbia, my graduate career was pretty typical for students looking to go into traditional academic teaching jobs, and no classes were oriented toward museum work in any specific way.

My early experience in the museum world reveals some interesting aspects of museum anthropology. **Most professional anthropologists in museums today are archaeologists—approximately 60 percent of museum curators are archaeologists, 30 percent are cultural anthropologists, and 10 percent are physical anthropologists.** There are probably a couple of reasons for this pattern. First, museums continue to sponsor a large volume of basic and contract archaeological research. Second, there has been a **natural affinity between archaeologists and museums for the past century because both have focused on material culture.** However, at the same time, at the Field Museum and many other anthropology museums, **comparatively little of what we do in terms of public programs and exhibits is directly related to archaeology. Most of it is ethnographically oriented depictions of non-Western cultures—the exotic "other."**

The other insight to be gained from my early career is that my role as an anthropologist in a museum had very little to do with the role of the institution as a museum per se. **I had no experience or exposure to the development of exhibits or public programs or in the care and**

maintenance of collections. I was a museum anthropologist only in the sense that a museum was the institutional sponsor of my archaeological fieldwork. I had no background, training, or knowledge of what a museum could or should be doing as a forum for public learning about anthropology. **For me, museums were vehicles for *doing anthropology,* not for *communicating anthropology.***

Following graduate school, I went on to a traditional teaching job and from there to a research/administrative position at a center for advanced studies in anthropology. My administrative experience in the latter setting eventually landed me an administrative job at the Field Museum, overseeing research and collections. I resigned that position several years ago to return full-time to anthropology as the museum's curator of North American anthropology.

In assuming the mantle of a full-time curator in a large museum, I have felt obliged to reexamine the role of the museum as a vehicle for communicating anthropology to a broad public audience. There is a tension today between the growing imperative to make anthropology relevant and an incongruous tendency to belittle the efforts of those who attempt to popularize disciplinary insights. **Perhaps the biggest challenge in getting the message of anthropology out to a broad public audience is one of language. Within the academy we speak our own language—*hermeneutics, commodification, processualism, avunculocality, proxemics,* and so on into the dim night. Outside of the academy, people do not understand this language.** Those who attempt to popularize anthropology must then translate the language, and, as in any translation, the nuance of meaning is often lost. But academicians thrive on nuance. They debate it, extol it, revel in it. Those who dare to ignore the nuance are thus seen, at least by some, as betraying the purity of the field.

Much is actually being done already to redress the problem of popularizing anthropology today. The American Anthropological Association, for example, annually honors individuals for carrying the message of anthropology to the public. Generally, I see this as a case of evolution in action. As the field comes under economic and intellectual stress in the environments of universities and funding agencies, it is going to have to find ways to better justify its existence. **One of the key ways by which anthropology can survive and thrive in the near future will be to win the interest, respect, and support of a broad public audience.** I believe that museums are a prime vehicle for gaining such support; however, I also think we are going to see changes in traditional teaching departments as more value is placed on talent for reaching the public through various media.

If museums are to be effective as institutions for communicating anthropology to a public audience, then museum curators have a much bigger responsibility today than just curating collections. They play the lead role in the museum as the people responsible for defining and articulating the knowledge and insights of anthropology to the interested visitors. Curators at the dawn of the 21st century, thus, need to have diverse qualities. **As curator, my own responsibilities at the Field Museum are divided into a broad range of tasks related to research, collections, and public education:**

- A key part of my job is to engage in **active anthropological research.** In my case, I am just finishing a long-term research project with my wife and colleague, Winifred Creamer, investigating the demographic dynamics of the Pueblo people of New Mexico during the contact period (approximately A.D. 1450 to 1680). We are also just initiating a new project on the coast of Peru. Generally, we spend every summer in the field actively involved in surveying, mapping, excavating, and examining collections in other museums. During the rest of the year I oversee analysis of materials recovered during the field season and participate in the process of writing up the results, as both editor and author. One big advantage of engaging in field research in a museum setting is that there is a formal publication venue, in this case Fieldiana: Anthropology, for publishing descriptive field reports that are often difficult to publish through traditional academic presses.
- Fieldwork is the romance and glory of the museum curator, but other parts can be equally challenging and productive. **Many of the traditional responsibilities of the curator for collections care have been taken over by specialized professional staff. Collections, however, still demand curatorial attention.** Using mostly federal grant monies (e.g., from the National Science Foundation, National Endowment for the Humanities, and National Park Service), I am in the midst of a ten-year project to consolidate and provide basic conservation maintenance (shelf liners, acid-free packing materials, etc.) for the entire anthropology collection of over 600,000 objects. This involves a close collaboration with the museum's conservator, registrar, and collection managers. Curatorial input on this project involves making decisions about arrangement of objects and collections, making collections more "user friendly" for visiting researchers, and addressing cultural concerns of native people represented in the collection.
- Beyond collections I play a both **proactive and reactive role in the public programs of the museum.** Proactively, I have presented a proposal for a complete revision of the museum's antiquated Halls of the Americas. Some exhibits in these halls date to the original opening of the museum in 1893, and all of them present an out-of-date, essentialist view of non-Western cultures, that is, the belief that there is an "essence" of Hopi culture, for example, that can be represented through dioramas and exhibits. The exhibits are dense with artifacts and depict Indian peoples of the Americas as an exotic "other" to be viewed across panes of glass by a visiting public in implicit alliance

with the institution of the museum. **My proposal would abandon the culture-specific exhibit format and use the halls as vehicles to communicate broad principles of anthropology.** One hall would be devoted to an exploration of the "complexification" of cultural systems from relatively simple hunting and gathering societies to much larger, denser, complex state and imperial polities. The Americas would be used as the platform for the exhibit, but it would not include expansive descriptions of cultural-historical sequences of area after area. A second hall would be devoted to the art and achievements of native peoples of the Americas. This hall will be largely curated by Native American artists and craftspeople and will draw heavily from our extensive collections from throughout the Americas. The third hall will be devoted to broad anthropological issues, such as migration, physical and cultural diversity, war, and the dynamics of demography. Contemporary people of the Americas—Western and non-Western—will be used as examples but will not be the focus of the exhibit per se.

Large, semipermanent exhibits are only one part of the public programs of a museum, however. We also mount a wide variety of visiting exhibits, sponsor public lectures, host local conferences, and participate in educational programs of Chicago and suburban public schools. The text and goals of these alternative types of public programming are set outside of the museum's academic departments, and my involvement as an anthropology curator is to review the accuracy of the anthropological content and confirm whether particular programs are in accord with the overall mission of the museum.

In some ways, **the position of museum curator is struggling for an identity as we approach the 21st century.** Most curators in museums today are archaeologists, and most are actively engaged in field research projects. Another substantial contingent is composed of cultural anthropologists working on material culture studies. The question in my mind is **how to transform both the image and the reality of professional anthropologists working in museums from "curators of collections" to "communicators of anthropology."** This transformation of the role of museum anthropologists will involve a number of changes in museum culture, and the curator of the 21st century will need to have diverse qualities:

1. **Museum anthropologists must excel at the delicate task of public communication.** Museums should be seen as havens for that somewhat beleaguered minority of anthropologists committed to carrying anthropology to a broad public audience. In the lofty world of academe, scholars who communicate effectively with the public are all too often belittled, disparaged, secretly envied, and marginally tolerated. Yet such individuals represent one of the few hopes for gaining public recognition and appreciation for the importance of anthropology in the modern world. Museums as

forums of informal public education are the perfect homes for anthropologists who have both the desire and the ability to carry anthropology to a public audience.

2. Museum curators will have to be able to **provide broad intellectual leadership within the museum to articulate and advocate the knowledge, findings, insights, and messages of contemporary anthropology.** Anthropology is by no means a unified discipline, and it will never be possible for a museum curatorial faculty to fully represent the field's range. However, the key here is not that museum anthropologists be able to cover all the bases but that they must be able to convey contemporary anthropology to an outside public and also serve as advocates of anthropology within the institution of the museum. The curatorial faculty have to provide leadership and direction not just for exhibits but also for educational programming for children and teachers, adult learning, community outreach, lecture series, and in-house publications. Museums, in turn, have to accept the anthropological leadership of the curators in areas that have increasingly been taken over by subfield specialists such as museum educators and exhibit developers.

3. The third role of the museum curator is an **active involvement in research programs.** Researchers involved in "doing" anthropology stay engaged with the discipline at large and can bring that engagement to bear on representing anthropology in museum contexts. Without the stimulation of students and the pressures of preparing lectures, museum curators can be isolated from the dynamics of change in the field. An active research program thus serves to directly connect the curator with the anthropological community at large and at the same time provides a sense of vibrancy to the anthropological program within the sometimes insulated world of the museum itself.

Overall, **museums today and the anthropology practiced in museums are in desperate need of redefinition.** They have been struggling along for far too long on collections from 100 years ago and trafficking in the exhibition of the world's cultural exotica. Simultaneously, the field of anthropology has grown increasingly detached from the general public and has lost the support of that public. In the face of these parallel dilemmas, the 21st century offers a unique opportunity for representing anthropology to a vast public audience. To take advantage of this opportunity, however, the practice of anthropology in museums is going to have to change, and there must be a reestablishment of the museum as a public voice for contemporary anthropology.

New entry, spring 1998
Revised, summer 1999

A Public Archaeologist in a Public Agency

Francis P. McManamon
National Park Service

A government archaeologist can do many things, in several different senses. One might work at the federal, state, or local level of government, each of which presents special challenges. One might find oneself doing fieldwork and analysis most of the time, or overseeing the work of archaeological contractors and coordinating work with others, or developing policies and regulations at the national, state, or local level. There is a **great variety in the kinds of activities that government archaeologists are involved in.** My job combines some of these different kinds of activities. I am the chief archaeologist of the National Park Service (NPS) and also serve as the departmental consulting archaeologist for the entire Department of the Interior, carrying out responsibilities assigned by several statutes to the secretary of the interior. Within the central office of the NPS, I also manage and supervise other anthropologists and archaeologists in the Archaeology and Ethnography Program of the service's National Center for Cultural Resource Stewardship and Partnerships in Washington, D.C. So, with this trio of titles, **what is the actual job that I do, and how did I come to it?**

First, let us look at the three titles and describe the work they involve. The Chief Archaeologist of the National Park Service works in the headquarters office of the park service in Washington, D.C. **The chief archaeologist serves as the primary adviser to the director of the NPS and other senior officials of the organization on activities and issues relating to archaeology.** For example, I develop national policies and guidelines for how archaeological sites and collections are treated. I recommend how funds for archaeological investigations are distributed nationally to other NPS offices. The job does not involve conducting archaeological field investigations or what normally is considered archaeological research. **The NPS employs about 125 full-time archaeologists.** Most of these professionals work at archaeological centers (located in Lowell, Massachusetts; Valley Forge, Pennsylvania; Tallahassee, Florida; Lincoln, Nebraska; Santa Fe, New Mexico; and Tucson, Arizona), regional offices, or national park units, for example, Gettysburg National Military Park, Hopewell Culture National Historical Park, Mesa Verde National Park, and North Cascades National Park.

The programs and projects for which the chief archaeologist is responsible focus on the development of policy, regulations, and guidance for national park system archaeology and the care of archaeological resources in NPS units. One of the activities related to this function involves working with other NPS archaeologists at the headquarters office and throughout the nation on **deciding how the $2.3 million available for archaeological inventory and recording of NPS archaeological sites is spent.** Another activity involves working with other archaeologists to develop a professional handbook describing archaeological methods and techniques to be used for various kinds of archaeological activities undertaken in NPS units.

The second title, **Departmental Consulting Archaeologist (DCA),** has a wider, government-wide scope. The title was **originally created in 1927** by the secretary of the interior to designate one archaeologist in the Department of the Interior who would **review applications for Antiquities Act permits and monitor the archaeological and paleontological work carried out under permits that were issued by the Department of the Interior.**

Jesse Nusbaum, the first NPS archaeologist in the southwestern United States, who also served at various points in his career as director of the Laboratory of Anthropology, Museum of New Mexico in Santa Fe, and as superintendent of Mesa Verde National Park, was designated the first DCA. Nusbaum reviewed all Antiquities Act permits and regularly visited the excavation sites, monitoring how the work was being conducted. In a series of reports to the secretary of the interior, he notes difficulties in the enforcement of the Antiquities Act, which prohibited excavation or removal of archaeological resources without the permission of the secretary. He notes increasing interest in American antiquities, the greater access to American archaeological sites because of the automobile, and the likelihood of tourists picking up artifacts as mementos. The issues in the **reports of 1929–31 resound to us in the 1990s when the looting of archaeological sites and the effects of cultural tourism continue to be of concern.**

The job of DCA has shifted and grown since 1927. Rather than reviewing and monitoring archaeological permits, **the job today involves coordinating archaeological programs administered and carried out by a variety of federal agencies, working on various archaeological initiatives and projects, and representing archaeological interests in planning, policy development, and other departmental activities.** This often is done through the drafting and enforcing of regulations and guidelines implementing laws that relate to archaeological resources, such as the Archaeological Resource Protection Act, the National Historic Preservation Act, and the Native American Graves Protection and Repatriation Act.

The final title, **Manager of the Archaeology and Ethnography Program at the NPS National Center for Cultural Resource Stewardship**

and Partnerships, is a more bureaucratic title. Federal agencies go through reorganizations regularly. The most recent for the NPS involved substantial "downsizing and restructuring" that moved personnel out of the central offices and into field positions. In the reorganization, the NPS combined its headquarters' functions related to NPS system archaeology, NPS system cultural anthropology, and the DCA function. All of these functions now are carried out by the **Archaeology and Ethnography Program. The program, located in Washington, D.C., has a staff of 14: seven archaeologists, three cultural anthropologists, three clerks or secretaries, and one editor.** In addition, there are seven consultants who work on program activities regularly and a number of student interns who spend a semester, a summer, or a year working on different activities.

Overall, the Archaeology and Ethnography Program carries out a variety of activities. One of these is providing professional anthropological and archaeological advice—what we often refer to as technical assistance to parks or offices within the NPS or other public agencies. Substantial amounts of energy and time are devoted to information exchange, including both a quarterly newsletter, *Common Ground,* and a series of technical publications on archaeological and cultural anthropological topics. Development and maintenance of the National Archaeological Database and a variety of interagency cooperative activities are carried out. As part of the national office of the NPS and Department of the Interior, we help to develop, review, and interpret national policies, regulations, and guidelines, as well as assist in liaison with Congress, other government departments, and private citizens and organizations. One area of particular concern during the past several years has been improving public understanding of, appreciation for, and participation in legitimate archaeological activities. A prominent component of this program is the series of activities undertaken to improve the protection of archaeological resources, as provided for by a number of statutes.

The DCA also has been assigned a variety of tasks related to the implementation of the Native American Graves Protection and Repatriation Act. Such tasks include drafting the regulations implementing the law, providing staff and professional support for the federal advisory committee established by the law, and administering grants to Indian tribes and museums.

Readers might justifiably ask **what kind of professional training would prepare one for the variety of work activities** summarized in the preceding paragraphs. Of course, there is no specific training course for any particular job, but there are certain general educational and professional experiences that are very helpful for jobs like mine. First, let me establish the baseline of educational training. I was trained as an archaeologist, with an A.B. from Colgate University (1973) where my course work included both sociology and anthropology courses, with a concentration on archaeological courses and an interest in European prehistory. I received both an M.A. (1975) and a Ph.D. (1983) from the State University of New York (SUNY) at Binghamton. In graduate school, I worked as a researcher for a public archaeology highway project and other public development projects in central New York. My original focus was in Western Europe, and I actually began my graduate career conducting research on European prehistory and doing fieldwork in the Netherlands. However, after focusing on this area for a year, I realized that the research problems in which I was most interested, hunter-gatherer studies within a settlement-subsistence evaluation framework (which were "hot topics" at that time), could also be addressed in northeastern North America with much less logistical difficulty. My graduate research for the M.A. involved hunter-gatherer adaptations in temperate environments, ethnohistoric studies of Native American adaptations in temperate environments, and quantitative and use-wear analysis of lithic assemblages.

After completing my M.A. at SUNY–Binghamton, I decided to explore whether or not I actually could get a job as a professional archaeologist. This is not a field that runs in my family or in any other families that I had been familiar with before graduate school, so some investigation seemed warranted. I had completed almost all of my required course work by then and had not yet begun my Ph.D. research. This turned out to be a good time to explore the employment environment.

During my second year in graduate school, I became interested in public archaeology, which was beginning to be a major topic in U.S. archaeology at that time. I worked as the archaeological lab director for public archaeology projects being done by faculty and students at the university. **I was fortunate in having at SUNY–Binghamton faculty members like Albert Dekin, Margaret Lyneis, Fred Plog, and Chuck Redman, who were interested in the professional potential of cultural resource management (CRM),** as it then was coming to be called. Lyneis, one of the early experts in CRM, taught a survey course and seminar in CRM, both of which I took. To explore job possibilities, I wrote to various state historic programs that I knew about, asking whether they were hiring archaeologists. I had a positive response from Massachusetts and, after two interviews, was hired in February 1976 as staff archaeologist for the Massachusetts Historical Commission, the Massachusetts State Historic Preservation Office (SHPO). It turned out that **I was the first professional archaeologist employed by the state.** Prior to my hiring, all archaeological advice had come from the state archaeologist, a retired, distinguished avocational archaeologist, Maurice Robbins. In my new job, I provided archaeological advice and guidance for the state office. A main part of the job was to review public projects to determine whether or not archaeological investigations ought to be done as part of the project and to review any archaeological work done for these projects. I also was responsible for updating and reorganizing the state archaeological site files. During this period, several federal and state agencies were involved with highway projects and environmental projects. A major part of the SHPO archaeologist's job was to work with professional staff of these agencies and convince them of their responsibilities to carry out the required archaeological research for their public projects.

In spring 1977, I learned that the NPS regional office in Boston was advertising a new job for regional archaeologist and I applied. In September 1977, **I was hired by the park service as the regional archaeologist for the North Atlantic region of the NPS, which covered New England, New Jersey, and New York.** In this position, I provided professional archaeological advice to the regional director and his staff in Boston. I also carried out small archaeological investigations at parks in the region, such as Minute Man National Historical Park, Saratoga National Historical Park, and Saugus Ironworks National Historical Site. For larger archaeological projects, contracts with consulting firms or universities were used, and the technical review of the work was my responsibility. For a few projects, notably a park-wide survey of Cape Cod National Seashore, I hired additional archaeological staff and carried out the investigation directly.

Working at the regional level for the NPS, I found that coordinating other professionals in planning, natural sciences, interpretation, law enforcement, and other fields was essential to achieve archaeological goals. If archaeological studies were to be done, they needed to be seen as important to the planners and to the park superintendent and staff. My professional recommendation was important, but I also had to articulate in more general terms why certain studies were needed, why certain sites were important, and why various actions were appropriate ones for archaeological preservation or protection rather than others. Put more simply, **the rationale supporting the proper actions to reach appropriate archaeological outcomes had to be argued for effectively without lapsing into jargon or simplistic reference to archaeological expertise.**

I also learned some things about scheduling, developing programmatic and project budgets, understanding and implementing laws and regulations, and other bureaucratic tricks of the trade. I was fortunate in having had Margaret Lyneis's CRM course and seminar, which had introduced such topics. The early years of my NPS career gave me opportunities to develop expertise and deepen my understanding of these important management topics.

While working as NPS regional archaeologist, I was able to complete the requirements for entrance to the Ph.D. program at SUNY–Binghamton and identify a research project that could serve as a Ph.D. dissertation topic. Again I was fortunate in having a Ph.D. committee at Binghamton, chaired by Al Dekin, that was supportive of my decision to continue to work professionally and to use an NPS archaeological project as a dissertation topic. It took nearly a decade from completing the M.A. to completing my

Ph.D. During that span, a number of Binghamton faculty served on my committee, including Al Ammerman, Meg Conkey, John Fritz, Chuck Redman, and Vin Steponaitis. In Boston, I also was fortunate in working for an associate regional director, Charlie Clapper, who was willing to have me spend part of my job time doing archaeological research needed for the NPS project that also could be used for my Ph.D. requirements. Of course, most of the research and writing that I did for my dissertation was done after work hours and on weekends and holidays. In the profession of anthropology and archaeology, getting ahead requires a willingness to spend the extra time doing these sorts of things.

Working at the regional level for the NPS also provided opportunities to become involved in national NPS archaeological activities. There were annual meetings of NPS archaeologists and other CRM professionals to plan national programs. There were special task forces to develop guidelines and policies or on other topics with a national scope. These experiences provide opportunities to meet colleagues from other parts of the country, as well as to learn about different perspectives on archaeological topics and concerns. It is possible to identify circumstances that are of national concern, as well as those that have special significance for different regions of the country. I find this particularly important in my own professional development as a means of developing new ideas and approaches to problems I face in archaeological or administrative matters.

In July 1986, I transferred to the Washington office of the NPS as chief of the Archaeological Assistance Program and began a program of working with other federal and state agencies, as well as private archaeological organizations, for the protection, preservation, and interpretation of archaeological sites throughout the United States. This job eventually led to the positions that I currently hold.

New entry, spring 1998 and summer 1999

Update on Projects Recovery and CONNECT

Merrill Singer
Hispanic Health Council

In 1993, seven years ago, I was interviewed by NAPA about my work and experiences as a professional anthropologist. The next several paragraphs contain a snapshot of two of the main projects I was involved in at the time, as reported verbatim in the original NAPA interview. A notable commentary on the sometimes fast-paced life of anthropologists whose primary work sites are outside of the university—in my case, in the impoverished inner city of Hartford, Connecticut—is the fact that I am no longer working on either of the projects described in my NAPA interview. Happily, since this piece was written, Project CONNECT has been refunded and is now operating under the banner of Project CONNECT 2000. The reasons for this change are discussed afterward, by way of introduction to update the set of projects I am working on today.

Seven Years Ago

Project Recovery, while it still continues in limited form, fell victim to the lack of adequate local funding available to maintain an innovative, culturally sensitive, and comprehensive drug treatment program. Project CONNECT suffered a similar cutback when Congress significantly reduced the budget of our funding agency, the Center for Substance Abuse Treatment. A lesson gained in both of these projects is that **ongoing interventions that address chronic health problems such as substance abuse are not easily sustained with time-limited grant dollars.** Funders commonly seek to launch new initiatives rather than to pick up and sustain established efforts. Change in health care funding, especially the introduction of managed care, also contributed to the problems encountered in both Project Recovery and Project CONNECT. Barred from receiving managed care payment for its case management services, **the Hispanic Health Council was forced to negotiate with a local hospital to take over Project Recovery as a sharply curtailed, institutionally based drug treatment program.** An important product of our work in drug treatment for pregnant women, however, was the opening of a residential drug treatment facility for this population by a local drug treatment provider. We continue to provide case management services for this program. Fortunately, two of the community-based organizations that participated in Project

CONNECT were able to get funding from the Connecticut Department of Public Health to continue providing a bridge to drug treatment services similar to those offered in the parent project. Thus, in evolved form, Projects Recovery and CONNECT have been able to make ongoing contributions to responding to the problems of drug dependency. I am proud of what we accomplished in these two projects, although comprehensive drug treatment (pretreatment through aftercare) remains an unfilled need.

Today

In the seven years since the NAPA interview, I have continued to work at the Hispanic Health Council, where I serve as associate director and chief of research. During the ensuing period, the council has grown in size, purchased its own building on Main Street in Hartford, and significantly expanded its research effort. My own work continues to focus on substance abuse and AIDS–related issues. Currently, I am helping to direct four different studies that are designed to improve our understanding of drug use and AIDS.

The first of these studies focuses on the issue of violence in the lives of drug users. Over the last decade, **violence has come to be recognized as a major public health issue.** Existing research suggests a significant relationship between violence and drug/alcohol use among both victims and perpetrators, with notable ethnic, age, and gender differences in the patterning of associations. There are also indications that **violence, as a force in community disruption and distrust, contributes to AIDS risk among substance users and, conversely, that fear of AIDS and the structure of relations in AIDS risk behavior may contribute to interpersonal violence.** In short, violence, drug/alcohol abuse, and AIDS emerge as three mutually reinforcing threats to the health and well-being of many people, especially in inner-city minority communities. The exact nature of the interrelationships among these three conditions, however, remains to be clarified; but there is little doubt that better understanding of these connections is critical to the development of effectively targeted prevention efforts. Vital in this regard is the development of a holistic approach that recognizes that **individual life experience and behavior do not unfold in a vacuum but, rather, are nested within a wider social/political/economic context of threats, resources, and opportunities.** Given the important knowledge gaps on drug-related/HIV–related violence, there is a critical need for basic epidemiological and community-based ethnographic research.

Based on our ongoing work in substance abuse and AIDS prevention research in the Puerto Rican community of Hartford, I helped to develop and am the principal investigator on Project SAVA, which is designed to examine specific relationships between *violence* (incidence, kind, victimization/perpetration, severity, psychological impact), *drug/alcohol use* (quantity, frequency, kind, method of consumption), and *AIDS risk* (injection drug use, noninjection drug use, sex related). This project is now in its final year. Already we are beginning to see how various forms of violence structure the lives of many of our participants, although we are finding that intensive life history interviewing across several sessions provides a much better window on the pervasiveness of violence than traditional epidemiological interviewing using forced-choice instruments.

Another set of new studies was developed under the auspices of the Yale Center for Interdisciplinary Research on AIDS and the Institute for Community Research. The first of these studies is a second-generation evaluation of the contributions of syringe exchange to AIDS prevention. A number of studies, including our own National Institute on Drug Abuse–funded evaluation of the Hartford Needle Exchange Program, have demonstrated the clear **AIDS prevention benefits from syringe exchange out into the wider networks of drug users who do not use the exchange program.** This study is being conducted in Hartford, Chicago, and Oakland. The second study examines AIDS risk in drug use settings (places people go specifically to consume drugs) and among networks of drug users who use such settings. Ultimately, the project is designed to assess the potential to implement prevention efforts in natural drug use locations. While initially intending to study both shooting galleries and crack houses, we found that such "thoroughbred" drug use settings are rare. Rather, **mixed forms of drug consumption in an array of different types of settings appear to be the norm in Hartford.**

The final study monitors changing patterns of drug use and AIDS risk behavior and seeks to rapidly identify and develop prevention responses to emergent risk behaviors. Currently, the project is focusing on the **smoking of "illies" (cigars that contain marijuana laced with embalming fluid). We are finding that this increasingly popular practice is associated with loss of judgment that seems to put users at special risk for automobile or other accidents.**

While focusing on somewhat different issues than Project Recovery and CONNECT, **the new projects continue my personal commitment to putting anthropological skills and insights to use in addressing the intertwined AIDS and drug use epidemics.** Over the last 20 years, I have seen that anthropologists have much to offer in this regard and that, as a result, a growing list of anthropologists has been able to play a role in shaping prevention and treatment efforts in the United States and internationally. Building effective responses to drug dependency and AIDS risk unavoidably requires staying close to the ground so as to be keenly aware of the changing patterns of day-to-day, situationally and culturally shaped behavior, a job that is well suited to the experience-near orientation of our discipline.

Originally appeared in Anthropology Newsletter, *October 1993*
Revised, spring 1998 and summer 1999

What Your Adviser Will Never Tell You

Susan Squires
GVO Inc.

I am a practicing anthropologist. In the three years since I received my Ph.D. in cultural anthropology (1990), I have been applying the theories and methods of anthropology to the challenges of educational reform in the United States. During this time I have come face to face with the fundamental problems encountered by the novice practicing anthropologist. I discovered the following:

- Anthropology is a great mystery to professionals in other disciplines; they don't have the foggiest idea what anthropologists think or do.
- As an anthropologist trained in a graduate program geared toward preparing students for teaching, I was unsure how to apply my anthropological training outside of academia. **I didn't have the foggiest idea what "practicing anthropologists" thought or did.**

In my struggle to define and explain the value of anthropology to others and myself, I learned two important lessons. I learned the need to translate anthropological theory to nonanthropologists so they could understand my work and make connections to their own work. I learned to translate anthropological methods so that others could use my work. I learned to value anthropology for its basic principles of holism and relativism, principles I had taken for granted. Plus I learned to value myself as a practitioner who could apply the theories of anthropology to a problem and suggest practical solutions. These are simple lessons, but lessons that took time to learn.

My academic training in anthropology provided me with a solid foundation grounded in the fundamentals of anthropological theory: the concept of culture, a holistic perspective, systems analysis, and training in the Western scientific method. This theoretical approach is the unique domain of anthropology and the fundamental core of training for an anthropologist no matter what career an anthropology student may contemplate.

Although I was trained in a "traditional" Ph.D. program (Boston University) geared toward preparing students for academic careers, I knew that teaching in an academic setting was not the career path I wished to pursue. While working toward my degree, I supported my studies by working as a planner in human services. I discovered that I really enjoyed the problem-solving aspect that this work provided, and I was determined to use my anthropological training in the private sector when I graduated. But what options did I have?

The NAPA Mentor Program was one source of information that I found helpful. At the time I graduated from Boston University, the NAPA Mentor Program was new, designed to assist "preprofessionals" who were interested in practicing anthropology. Although I did not know it at the time, **I became the first "preprofessional" in the program.** I was unsure exactly what the program could offer, and the funding members of the program were unsure about what support "preprofessionals" would need. Nonetheless, it was a good match. Through my mentor, Cathleen Crain of LTG Associates, I received advice and support in preparing a résumé and networking. I also gained a friend and colleague.

In 1992 I joined The Network, Inc., a private nonprofit organization. This is an organization dedicated to educational improvement and reform. Another anthropologist, Sarah C. Uhl, soon joined me. At the time Uhl and I were hired, The Network had been awarded funding to undertake an investigation of educational reform efforts in the northeastern United States. **We were hired because we were anthropologists and anthropologists "do" ethnography.** The Network needed people to "do" ethnographies of schools, school districts, and other educational sites where educational reform was planned. Those who are involved in educational research value ethnographic work, and anthropologists are valued for the contribution they can provide to further such work. Both Uhl and I soon learned that our value as anthropologists began and ended with ethnography. Yet we have been able to contribute much more to our "employer."

The Network had a strong focus on serving its clients. To me this focus felt natural. Anthropology is grounded in the need to understand the "other" and the point of view of others. Anthropologists have traditionally not labeled the "other" as "client," but the principle is the same. **To be able to identify the needs and assumptions of the "other" (or in this case, the clients) is a valuable skill.** Yet this is a skill that the nonanthropologist finds hard to develop. It is valued in those who can do it.

Understanding systems and systems change is another area where we have been able to contribute to an understanding of educational reform in ways that others with training in other disciplines have not. An approach to understanding culture is important in understanding systems. Understanding systems, organizations, and complex change is an important contribution that the anthropologist can make not only in education but also in business and government.

It is satisfying that I work in an organization that has another anthropologist. I have a colleague who shares a knowledge base with me, and we have used this common theoretical foundation to conduct several joint research projects of our own. Most recently we have been conducting research on collaboration. This research has grown from the work we have undertaken in educational reform and rehabilitation and has led us to develop a model of collaboration based on process (and very unlike the static models currently in vogue in education, social services, and business). We presented this model of collaboration at the 1993 American Anthropological Association Annual Meeting in Washington, D.C.

Working in the private sector has not limited our ability to undertake anthropological research, although it has structured it differently. Both of us feel that we are "doing" more with anthropology than we ever would have done in our previous experience as university professors. My own knowledge and appreciation of anthropology, anthropological theory, and the value of anthropology as a discipline has grown because of the opportunity to apply anthropological thinking in the private sector.

Addendum to the Original Practitioner Profile

The practitioner profile that I wrote in March 1994 reflects observations and experiences that have only been amplified over the intervening four years. Anthropology continues to be a mystery to most of the professionals in other disciplines with whom I have now had the opportunity to work.

In 1995 I was asked to join Andersen Consulting/Arthur Andersen as their "resident anthropologist" at the Center for Professional Development in St. Charles, Illinois. **"At last," I thought, "an organization with the sophistication to know about anthropologists and the contribution that anthropology can bring to the business environment."** In some respects this hope was realized. They were particularly interested in my ability to conduct qualitative research. I began at Andersen by evaluating the effectiveness of training provided at the center where I was located.

Training participants came from all parts of the world. Many of the staff based at the center recognized the importance of providing effective training to participants regardless of their home countries. Such research was usually undertaken using standardized survey techniques. It was common for training participants to complete a training evaluation questionnaire at the end of a course. Results were primarily quantitative. It was recognized that I had a special ability—attributable in their eyes to my qualitative evaluation skills, however, and not my anthropological training—to evaluate these courses.

If staff sought my help as an anthropologist, it was usually on an impromptu basis. People would come to me with questions such as, "I am meeting some clients from India. How should I greet them?" or "I just found out that I am going to Moscow next week. What should I do to prepare for this trip?" These "anthropology consultations" usually lasted about a minute and a half. At Andersen, anthropology primarily equated with good qualitative research—an accurate if limited understanding of the profession.

It was during a time of frustration with the slow progress of educating Andersen personnel about the usefulness of anthropology that a research and design firm in California approached me to become their "ethnographer." **"At last,"** I thought, **"an organization with the sophistication to know about anthropologists and the contribution that anthropology can bring to the business environment."** I have been in California about three years as of this writing. And while I find the perception of anthropology becoming more sophisticated, once again I am finding that the understanding of anthropology is limited. To those in the design field, anthropology means ethnography, and ethnography means context-based observation and interviews.

In the years since I received my degree in anthropology, I have been amazed at how much I continue to draw on my academic training. It provided me with a solid foundation in the fundamentals of anthropological theory and with the methodological tools necessary to be successful in a business environment. But I am also amazed and challenged by the need to continuously explain the breadth and depth of skills and knowledge that anthropology has to offer. While it is sometimes frustrating to do this, I realize that **my continued success and the success of business anthropology depends on the individual anthropologist's ability to combine good anthropology with the ability to translate, explain, and educate others about the profession itself.**

Originally appeared in Anthropology Newsletter, *March 1994*
"Addendum" text added, spring 1998
Revised, summer 1999

On the Road Again: International Development Consulting

Mari H. Clarke
USAID Office of Private/
Voluntary Cooperation

Mari Clarke with First Undersecretary of Education, Cairo, Egypt

My work as an international development consultant has led me to many countries over the past 18 years. This month I am in Albania; two months ago I was bouncing around in a Russian jeep in Mongolia, driving over frozen rivers and visiting *gers*—the round, portable homes of nomadic herders of sheep, goats, camels, yaks, and horses. My work has touched on various issues— natural resource management, maternal and child health and family planning, education, democracy, and small enterprise development, as well as national and international policies on the advancement of women. **The common theme has been the integration of a gender perspective into policies, programs, and projects: that is, a focus on the ways women's and men's roles affect their access to and benefits from development efforts.**

Since I began working in this field, attention to the human dimension has increased a great deal. The U.N. Development Program now advocates "human-centered development." The U.S. Agency for International Development (USAID) and the World Bank now emphasize "participatory development." However, there remains **a tendency to focus on the material rather than on the human side of development, such as the adjustment of the macroeconomy, the protection of trees in deforested areas, and the expansion of markets.** In addition, development programs are often compartmentalized into discrete "technical" sectors such as agriculture, natural resources, education, health, and finance.

In actual practice, it is the human factor that is essential to move along the goods and processes in all the sectors to achieve sustainable development. Anthropology makes a major contribution to international development with its holistic approach that examines links between "sectors" to understand how the "system" works. Particularly valuable is anthropology's emphasis on understanding local people's knowledge and perceptions and its methodologies for getting at those ideas. The triangulation of quantitative and qualitative methodologies is also important, as are fine-tuned skills in listening and observing.

My path to work in international development was an opportunistic one. I was an undergraduate major in anthropology at Michigan State University in the late 1960s. My focus was archaeology. During my graduate school work at the University of Pennsylvania, a course on "cultural ecology" with Robert Netting was a critical turning point in my career. It provided a practical analytical framework focused on the interrelationships among social organization, the economy, and the environment. This framework has evolved and guided my work over time. The course also provided me with an opportunity to do research for a regional archaeological project in Greece. I studied traditional agricultural technology and the farmers' use of the local environment and concluded that working with people was more to my liking than interpreting behavior through artifacts. I completed a master's thesis on wild plant use in the context of small holder farming.

I moved to North Carolina and worked for a policy research program on the impact of national policies on the American family. This sparked an interest in policy issues. After completing a Mass Media Fellowship sponsored by the American Association for the Advancement of Science, I decided to add another notch to my belt of qualifications. I completed a **master's degree in instructional media. It was this degree, rather than my anthropological credentials, that opened the door to international development work.** My entrée was a job as an instructional designer for a USAID–funded project on maternal and child health and family planning training in Africa and the Middle East. I trained nurse-midwives in how to design instructional materials and use visual aids effectively in Kenya, Egypt, Turkey, and Sierra Leone. I also enrolled in the graduate program in anthropology at the University of North Carolina at Chapel Hill. Toward the end of the five-year contract, I defended a proposal to conduct Ph.D. research in Kenya on household economics as a case study for the World Bank's housing project there.

In the meantime, **an opportunity arose to direct a project developing technical training materials for Peace Corps health volunteers in conjunction with the Center for Disease Control, the World Health Organization, and USAID.** I put my research grants on hold and headed to Chicago to work with the small consulting firm that had won the contract. By the time I returned from Chicago a year later, the World Bank had decided to drop the case study component of the research in Kenya. I revised and redefended my research proposal to return to Greece to look at household economics there, where I knew the language and the lay of the land.

When I was in Chapel Hill preparing to defend my dissertation, I received a call from the Office of Women in Development (WID) at USAID. That office was looking for a communications specialist. My résumé had been passed on by a colleague. After my interview with the director of the WID office, I was offered another position as labor specialist, based on my research experience. I joined the office in 1988 and worked there as an on-site consultant until 1996. Working on a crosscutting issue such as WID enabled me to learn a great deal about the workings of the development bureaucracy in USAID and other international donor and nongovernmental organizations (NGOs). I worked primarily on policy and strategic planning and evaluation. I assisted various parts of the organization to better integrate women into their efforts by understanding gender issues. **After the opening of former Soviet bloc countries, I provided technical assistance in the Balkans,** drawing on my dissertation fieldwork experience. I also served on the U.S. delegation to the European Preparatory Conference for the Fourth World Conference on Women.

 I left the USAID WID office in 1996 to direct an Education Secretariat Project that was part of the Gore-Mubarak Partnership for Economic Growth and Development. This entailed coordination with high-level policy makers in Egypt and the United States to exchange best practices in education and initiate activities to enable the Egyptian education system to prepare young people with skills needed to compete in the world economy in the 21st century. When the project ended, I moved into independent consulting, which brings me full circle to my recent trip to Mongolia on a social safety net project design team for the Asian Development Bank and my current work conducting a baseline survey on gender issues in forestry in Albania.

 The market for international development work has grown much tighter in the last decade as funds have been cut by the United States and other countries. Hence, it is much more difficult for people entering the field now than it was in the past. Experience is the most important key. Internships and volunteer work for NGOs and the Peace Corps provide valuable international experience that makes a difference on a résumé; USAID, the World Bank, and other organizations have young professionals' programs. Along with experience come contacts and opportunities for networking. **Active networking is essential to stay in touch with the international job market.** Professional associations such as the National Association for the Practice of Anthropology, the Society for Applied Anthropology, and the Washington Association of Professional Anthropologists provide valuable networking contacts and opportunities. Additional credentials in public health, law, international relations, or business increase credibility and provide an edge in a competitive consulting market. Because of the nature of the work, outstanding interpersonal skills are highly valued. Demonstrated ability to write clearly and concisely is also a great asset. Skills in foreign languages are also desirable.

Postscript, September 1999

 Shortly after completing this article, I accepted a position directing a project that provides program support to the USAID Office of Private and

Voluntary Cooperation (PVC). The PVC office provides funding and institutional capacity development assistance to grassroots organizations such as Save the Children, Freedom from Hunger, and Care. **Instead of traveling to distant lands, I am now hiring consultants to conduct evaluations of PVC grants around the globe.** The project also provides logistical and technical support to the Advisory Committee for Voluntary Foreign AID (ACVFA), a high-level group of leaders from the voluntary assistance community who advise the administrator of USAID. **Coming full circle to the gender focus of my work, one of the major studies that ACVFA is conducting, through our project, focuses on USAID progress in institutionalizing gender in its policies and programs.** I have the pleasure of working with a former ambassador to Nepal and a retired foreign service officer, whom I have hired to conduct the study. In addition to the consultants supporting the project, I also have a dynamic and dedicated young staff of former Peace Corps volunteers who provide daily support to the PVC office. I enjoy working with them to help solve problems and assisting them in fine-tuning their professional skills in international development.

New entry, spring 1998
Revised, summer 1999

Nonacademic Experience and Changing Views of the Discipline

Michael Painter
Wildlife Conservation Society/Bolivia

I received my Ph.D. in anthropology from the University of Florida in 1981 and went to the Institute for Development Anthropology (IDA) in January 1983. IDA is a nonprofit, tax-exempt research and educational institution that applies social science research to supporting the efforts of low-income populations to define and defend their rights to resources that are basic conditions of a secure and fulfilling life. Support for IDA research has come from bilateral and multilateral development agencies, governments, foundations, and individuals.

My own job has focused on establishing and building the IDA research program in Latin America. My other responsibility has been administering worldwide the major portion of our short-term technical services. Because we frequently contract social scientists and other professionals to conduct short-term assignments with the teams we field, this is the way that many professionals initially become acquainted with IDA.

The IDA Latin American program has focused on food and agriculture, the environment, and natural resources. The unifying theme is exploring how social relations that organize production shape people's use of land and other resources. Among the major projects we have undertaken is a five-year study of the production linkages between upland valleys and tropical lowland areas in Bolivia and the association of the production of coca leaf for cocaine with development policies that resulted in widespread rural impoverishment and subsidized capital accumulation by a small agroindustrial elite. A second five-year project in Bolivia has looked at gender issues associated with rural impoverishment and land degradation. Both of these studies, as well as other research, have been **conducted in collaboration with nongovernmental and grassroots organizations and, in some cases, with government agencies. We are currently preparing to undertake a long-term study of social conflicts associated with the establishment and management of protected areas in Ecuador, Peru, and Bolivia, which we will codirect with the Latin American Social Science Faculty** in Quito and environmental nongovernmental organizations in each of the three countries.

Several aspects of my job have been particularly important in shaping my perspective on the practice of anthropology. First, work at **IDA offers an unusual opportunity to move back and forth between academic and nonacademic domains.** We are first and foremost a research institute, and the research agendas of our directors and staff have shaped the experience of IDA. Thus, we are like academics in that a substantial amount of our self-image, the validation of the importance of our work, and the measures of our productivity are related to scholarly publications. I have also been fortunate to maintain an intellectually rewarding relationship with the State University of New York at Binghamton, teaching graduate seminars in the anthropology department and advising students in the anthropology and sociology programs. At the same time, our work is applied, and we see in ways that most of our academic colleagues do not the implications of social theories when they are applied in the context of political struggles.

One impact of this experience has been to make me **uncomfortable with discussions that tend to reify the distinction between anthropological theory and practice.** Too often, those of us who define our interests as applied evaluate social theory in light of its immediate relevance to so-called practical problems, without considering how and why those problems have been constructed as they have. Equally important, too often those of us who define our projects as theoretical decline to accept responsibility for how our perspectives are used by others and fail to recognize how our research agendas are influenced by relations of power that result in the market for particular kinds of ideas at particular times. These tendencies impede efforts to engage people in a critical discussion about the social processes that continually transform our world.

A second, related impact of my job has been that I have become **very aware of the political dimensions of practicing anthropology and of the complexities of political processes.** For example, **one cannot do research on land use without being confronted with very basic questions involving who defines and controls access to critical resources and whose access is restricted or, often, cut off altogether.** In societies in which people are divided and grouped together in intricate and contradictory ways by class, ethnicity, and gender, populist homilies about our first obligation being to the people studied, local people knowing best, and the advantages of local control over economic and political affairs tell us where our hearts should be but say little about what we need to do if our actions are to have the impact we say we want them to have. In any event, much of this discourse has been appropriated by institutions for which the well-being of poor people ranks near the bottom of their lists of concerns and which turn populist discourse against the poor in extraordinarily imaginative ways.

The contradictions that arise from this are never far from the minds of those who work with IDA. The ideal of social science supporting the efforts of poor and disenfranchised people to improve the quality of their lives was a central reason for founding IDA; it continues to shape our sense of who we are. But IDA is an independent institution with no endowment, and we rely on grants and contracts, many of which come from organizations whose records in the area of improving the well-being of the poor are mixed at best. The resulting **tension between the need to secure the financial resources to permit the institution to continue and the effort to remain true to the reasons why IDA was founded in the first place is something that everyone feels every day.**

There is no formula for resolving the tension. We all attempt to address it in our own work by using our social science skills to analyze an activity or potential activity in light of who stands to benefit and who stands to lose. We also try to act on the basis of our individual morality and political values. Sometimes we think we have been right, and sometimes hindsight shows us that our judgment was wrong. But there is never an activity in which we do not think carefully about what ends our work serves. Outsiders may not agree, and we may not agree among ourselves, that a particular decision was the right one. But the issue is always explicit, and our roles as individual actors and representatives of different sets of interests are always clear.

Our university-based colleagues, even those whose professional perspectives are critical, are often remarkably uncritical about the larger ends their work serves. This is possible because the impact of their work on the well-being of the institutions that support them is usually indirect, and they often do not see the impact of something they wrote or said about the people who were the subjects of their discussion. These complexities in the division of labor among social scientists obscure the fact that all of us, regardless of our institutional bases, are linked to those we study by social processes that shape our respective standards of living and create a market for what we teach and write. In this regard, I think **the current critical examination of development has great (but, as yet, largely unrealized) potential to clarify the nature and purpose of social science inquiry about the lives of relatively poor and powerless people.**

Addendum to Practitioner Profile

Since my practitioner profile was published in the November 1994 issue of the *Anthropology Newsletter,* my career has taken some turns that have led me to reflect on the remarks I make in the original piece. In December 1994, the month after my profile was published, I **accepted an offer from Chemonics International, a consulting firm based in Washington, D.C., to join a team implementing a community-based natural resource management project in Botswana.** I spent two and a half years in Botswana, where I was responsible for establishing a system to monitor the impact of the project on people's well-being and on how they use natural resources. Funded by the U.S. Agency for International Development (USAID), the project was, and continues to be, part of a broad effort by the government of Botswana and several international donors to bring together at the local level authority and responsibility for the management of Botswana's impressive wildlife resources. By creating conditions whereby people who live day to day with wildlife benefit economically from its conservation-oriented management, the project seeks to create incentives for them to conserve wildlife and the habitats on which different species depend.

Then, in July 1997, I had the opportunity to return to Bolivia as the chief-of-party of the Kaa-Iya Project, a joint activity of the Wildlife Conservation Society (WCS) and the Capitanía de Alto y Bajo Izozog (CABI), which is supported by a grant from the USAID. Subsequently, I also became the coordinator of the WCS overall program in Bolivia. My work in Bolivia has focused on two broad themes: (1) building grassroots technical and administrative capacity to promote conservation and manage natural resources based on concepts of sustainability and (2) addressing the challenges that changes in land use resulting from hydrocarbon development pose for the livelihoods of rural people and efforts to conserve critical habitats in eastern Bolivia.

CABI, WCS's partner in implementing the Kaa-Iya Project, is the traditional political organization for the Guarani people of Izozog, and its structure and forms of decision making date to their earliest recorded contracts with Europeans. As part of a strategy for defending their lands from an advancing agricultural frontier, CABI took the initiative to turn a substantial part of its historical territory into the Kaa-Iya del Gran Chaco National Park and Natural Areas for Integrated Management, within Bolivia's national protected area system. CABI administers the 3,400,000-hectare Kaa-Iya Protected Area, which is the largest of Bolivia's protected areas and the largest protected area containing dry tropical forest in the world. It is also the only protected area in the western hemisphere established as a result of the initiative of Native Americans and administered by them. WCS provided CABI with technical assistance in the preparation of its proposal to have the area declared protected. It continues to provide assistance as CABI strengthens its own technical and administrative capacity, and it works to integrate the management of the protected area with that of the rest of the Izoceño-Guaraní lands.

My work involving hydrocarbon development arose from the WCS collaboration with CABI and our efforts to support them as they sought to address the social and environmental impact of the construction of the Bolivia-Brazil Gas Pipeline. The pipeline is the largest energy-related project undertaken to date in South America, and it transverses the lands of the Izoceño-Guaraní, as well as those of the Chiquitano and Ayoreode peoples. It also crosses the Kaa-Iya Protected Area. With support from key officials at the World Bank, Inter-American Development Bank, and the Corporación Andina de Fomento, we were able to work with CABI to establish an agreement that (1) establishes a new organizational structure for indigenous people and the pipeline companies to define together the impacts that require attention and (2) provides an important source of funds to permit appropriate projects and programs to be designed and implemented. We have subsequently applied this experience in other settings, including a second pipeline to Brazil, which branches off the first pipeline and passes through the Chiquitano Forest, and two hydrocarbon exploration and exploitation concessions that the government of Bolivia has granted inside the Kaa-Iya Protected Area. Each of these settings has brought new challenges, and it remains to be seen if our efforts to address the impact of hydrocarbon development on the people and land of eastern Bolivia will be successful in any lasting way.

These jobs have brought changes to my perspective, based on my reduced participation in academic life. As I note in my original profile, IDA provided an unusual opportunity to move freely between academic and nonacademic settings. Since leaving IDA, my physical distance and limited opportunity for interaction with colleagues there have reduced my participation in university life. At the same time, I have **continued to have fairly steady contacts with colleagues and students for whom the projects in which I have been involved have been part of the raw material for their research.** I have benefited greatly from some of these exercises, which helped me to think about important issues in different ways and to maintain a critical perspective on my work.

The other big change I have experienced since leaving IDA has been working for institutions whose missions are not defined in terms of social science concerns. **At IDA, we did considerable multidisciplinary work, but the contributions of other disciplines tended to be measured in terms of the extent to which they enriched our worldviews as anthropologists. Now it is up to me to use anthropology to enrich the worldviews of professionals from other disciplines.**

One impact of this has been to make me **more critical of the assertions that anthropologists conventionally make about the benefits of our research among grassroots organizations.** For example, CABI recently received a research proposal from a well-respected social scientist who was interested in the role of traditional organization in reflecting and shaping the thinking about using natural resources of the Izoceño people the organization represents, as it makes decisions affecting their resource access. The topic appeared interesting and important, and CABI decided to consider offering the researcher an institutional affiliation. It referred the proposal to a committee that included indigenous leaders and technical advisers. I was one of the advisers asked to review and comment on the proposal. The proposal itself was similar to many that I have helped students that I worked with at Binghamton write and that I have reviewed favorably on behalf of different funding agencies with regard to the assertions contained about the relevance of the study and the benefits it would offer CABI and other grassroots organizations.

When the committee reviewed the proposal, it found that what the researcher wanted was for CABI to grant virtually unlimited access to its staff and its files, to help identify and contact people who would criticize the organization, and to provide transportation and logistical support. In return, the researcher would publish critical discussions about whether he thinks that CABI really does what it says it does or whether he thinks it is misleading itself and its constituency. While he would acknowledge CABI assistance, all publications would be in his name, and, because of his commitment to academic freedom, CABI would exercise no control over the content or the quality of his publications. The researcher also offered to organize critical public discussions about CABI at his university. While his funding did not allow him to provide any representatives of CABI with the resources to travel there, CABI officers were told that they would be welcome at the seminars if they could pay their own expenses.

The benefits to CABI were to be greater self-knowledge, based on the researcher's perspective as an outsider—trained in the analysis of levels of meaning—and the possibility of having others come, following in the wake of this research, to do similar, related studies. CABI informed the researcher that it was not in a position to host such a project at this time, and it suggested ways in which the researcher might refocus the project so that it would be able to offer an institutional affiliation. The initial reaction of the researcher was indignation at what he saw as the effrontery of CABI to criticize his proposal and its lack of respect for his academic freedom. To his credit, he did come to see that its concerns were not spurious, although he has not yet indicated whether he would be interested in reworking the project based on CABI's suggestions.

For the record, it is important to note that CABI's general posture is to encourage outside researchers who can bring a critical perspective to what it is doing. There are currently two doctoral students from U.S. universities completing their dissertation research with local institutional support from CABI and more than a half-dozen Bolivian students at the *Licenciatura* or master's level completing independent research on topics related to land and wildlife management. The difference is that these researchers made the effort to define specific ways that would support the CABI program by working issues of particular interest into their research designs and defining other areas in which they could provide services that CABI needs. That effort provided a framework of true reciprocity in which CABI had no difficulty in supporting their work as independent researchers.

The lesson I gleaned from this case is that **anthropologists need to be more aware of how our own role as observers may be perceived by those we observe, particularly when our proposals are based on assertions of solidarity with them and expressions of concern for their welfare.** We tend to see our role as observers as self-evidently good and our accounts of our observations as self-evidently beneficial. When our would-be subjects do not share that view, we tend to assume that they are threatened by what we might find. In the CABI case, no one who read the proposal was threatened in the least by the prospect of being observed. What CABI did perceive was that the research was going to demand a tremendous amount of time from busy people and that it offered little in return. To the extent that we are interested in bringing social theory to bear in ways that are of service to people engaged in struggles for the means to earn livelihoods or human rights, we need to look closely and critically at the processes that bring us and them together. We also need to think more than we usually do about what of ourselves and our work we are willing to offer in return for their collaboration.

Originally appeared in Anthropology Newsletter, *November 1994*
"Addendum" text added, spring 1998 and summer 1999

Reflections on Ethics Working in International Development

Wendy Wilson Fall
West African Research Center

A certain well-known, established anthropologist once brought me to tears on a train ride going south toward Washington, D.C. These were not tears of joy but, rather, of frustration and loss. The anthropologist will go unnamed; it is not important for the moment. I think it is more important to name the feelings that I had at that time—perhaps, indeed, even to name the moment itself. I hope this column will be a good place to tell the story and stimulate some discussion on the ethics of "applying" anthropology.

It was during this train ride that the aforementioned anthropologist told me that I had no place in academia, and I was urged to stay in my role as "an anthropologist who consults, who works in international development." **It was a moment of divergence between the concept of classical anthropology "in academe" and the concept of the "application" of anthropological knowledge and skill to assist people—and, simply, one's need to be employed.**

Up to that point in my career as an anthropologist, I had assumed that there was an operating thesis that was bigger than our chosen paths in anthropology (or in our individual lives). I believed that we shared a value of the study of human behavior—the significance of the science of anthropology. I had then, and still have, the notion that against all odds one should tenaciously hold onto the creed that the study of human interaction is worthwhile. People of diverse backgrounds ultimately have something to share, if only the shock and stimulation of seeing something or someone different from oneself. I had also believed that it was not dishonorable to attempt to get paid work that supports such a creed.

I lost something that day on the train. I lost a sense that as anthropologists we understood the other's métier; and I lost the comfortable feeling I had of assuming that anthropologists of whatever cultural background understand that a single mother has to work.

But I also held onto my beliefs. I still believe that it is okay to engage in actions for altruistic reasons. I also believe that it is okay to respond to the need to make money, support oneself, be responsible to one's children, and consider the integrity of what a mature adult must do along with the integrity of one's chosen discipline and how to practice it. In my view, neither the individual nor the discipline is diminished by this point of view. Human society—the world—is, in a way, the laboratory that puts our discipline to the test. We are constantly challenged by our assumptions and the questions posed by the anthropological enterprise, whether we are in "academe" or "applied."

It is the academic endeavor that brings rigor and necessarily more profound analysis to the issues and situations that have often been illuminated by the activity of applied anthropologists who attempt to describe and to affect the world in medias res (as things happen). Should one feel obligated to exercise only one or the other option and carefully avoid intellectual or behavioral "spillover" from one sector to the next? This question, raised for me in such harsh terms years ago, has not gone away. It was difficult then and it is difficult now.

Morality? Which aspect of morality and superior ethical position is relevant here? the superior integrity of committing oneself to the academic endeavor and not "sullying" oneself with too much money? the morality of not working as an academic in order to respond to other opportunities that pay better (not to mention the only ones available at the time) and render a single parent more able to provide family security? Or how about the altruistic impulse? the driving desire to make the world a better place, contribute something positive to transformations in human society that may help humans be better, do better? or saving something worthwhile that might otherwise be lost? an art, a craft, a way of doing things? All of these are questions likely to be important to social anthropologists and other people who are concerned with society and change and with learning and the pursuit of knowledge.

The problem comes, of course, when the contradictions between the practitioner's intentions and the working situation's context become bigger than the importance of the tasks at hand. I work as a paid technical assistant and team member, where we work on the goal of using the local dynamics of knowledge transfer for introducing new or altered technologies. But even within this research-oriented environment, these moral questions remain interior ones. They remain personal issues not easily transferable. They have been eclipsed, in reality, by the larger, more brutal universe of the current international character of technology. The means by which people have access to technology and the reasons for which they do not have effective technologies in the first place seem to have all but occluded any altruistic concerns about the value of diversity or exchange. I have found that the greater truth of the current configuration of power and influence in international development is finally becoming a serious bottleneck to growth and security and that the contradictions of the situation are apparent every day.

My sincerity as a social scientist or that of my fellow researchers cannot obfuscate the fact that right now **most bilateral agreements (government to government) for projects in Africa fail to recognize that there are likely many Africans who can fulfill these roles at less or equal cost.** They ignore professional resentment as well. The model I am operating within almost ignores local-level expertise. And yet Africa is beginning to resemble the image described by Eliot Berg, the economist, when he spoke of Asia. He pointed out that there comes a time when long-term technical assistance is no longer relevant, acceptable, or accepted. There is now a local pool of highly skilled workers only intermittently employed who can easily fill most positions needed for technical assistance in current development projects. It is clear that the place I am occupying could be filled by someone a little closer to the source. At the present time, the value that purportedly was brought to the situation in the form of "different perspectives, diverse experience" has been overrun by the immediate, unavoidable realities that this "differentness" is currently too expensive, in terms of labor deployment and budgets, for a developing country to stand for much longer.

But hey! Wait a minute! What about these altruistic notions of the value of the exchange of information, notions, perceptions? What role does an applied anthropologist have here? For me, it should still be good for foreigners from "there" to meet foreigners from "here." It is still worthwhile for different minds to work together to solve a mutually identified problem. It may be in some cases advantageous. What is clear, though, is that some operating assumptions have outlived their time.

Does this mean that I am even "dirtier" and more morally questionable than I ever thought I was? I don't think so. Is there no relationship between behavioral theory or world systems theory and this particular empirical field? I don't think so. Can questions posed in this situation somehow inform ongoing debates in academe? I certainly hope so. In fact, the work is not becoming less relevant, just harder. It is requiring more of us and more of the discipline.

Just as anthropologists often have been in the forefront in assisting "native" informants and their communities with access to better living conditions, to fight unjust laws or policies, or even to have the right to tell their stories, we continue to be challenged in new ways regarding the communities and persons with whom we collaborate and on whom very often our research depends. One way we can help in these times is to continue to be vocal about the importance of the applied experience and the lessons that are learned in that context.

At the time of this writing, I was employed as a long-term technical assistance provider with USAID and working at a national research institute. Since that time, I left to represent the National Council of Negro Women as their West African Regional Office director. This office assists in the implementation of community development projects funded from the exterior, usually the United States. As of October 1999, however, I will be taking the post of director of the West African Research Center, also funded in the United States. In each experience, the questions of parity and the desirability of cultural exchange are pertinent. Although each situation offers a different perspective, I am cognizant that certain issues remain.

Originally appeared in Anthropology Newsletter, *April 1996*
Revised, spring 1998 and summer 1999

Building a Bridge between Academics and Practice

Ann T. Jordan
University of North Texas

As an associate professor in the Institute of Anthropology at the University of North Texas, I am a **practicing anthropologist with an academic position.** The institute is in the School of Community Service, which is a school of applied social science. Consequently, we are well situated to advance our goal of conducting applied work in the academic setting.

My career has had some twists and turns not uncommon for practicing anthropologists. I received my Ph.D. in 1979 from the University of Oklahoma, an academic-oriented rather than applied-oriented graduate program. This traditional training has served me well. While I support the development of applied-oriented graduate programs, a solid traditional training provides the base in theory and method a practicing anthropologist needs. The advantage of an applied program is that it exposes the student to the rapidly expanding applied literature and focuses on those methods most appropriate for applied work. I spent the first ten years of my career working as an adjunct at a number of universities and coming to the realization that anthropologists have a responsibility to further the applied side of the discipline. **I believe that it is our ethical responsibility to use what we know to help solve human problems.**

As an academic/practicing anthropologist, **I consider it my role to bridge the gap between academics and practice.** My work includes both traditionally oriented research and applied projects. In traditionally oriented research, I try to bring the insights and theory development gained from applied work back into the academic arena; and in applied work, I try to contribute to the solution of real human problems using knowledge gained in traditional research.

My work is focused in two areas: organizational anthropology and American Indian studies. In the field of organizational anthropology, the possibilities for anthropology are so great that they seem endless. My work has focused on organizational culture and the use of anthropological theory and method to better understand how humans behave in complex organizational settings. For example, I am currently part of a multidisciplinary team at the University of North Texas that is studying leadership in work teams in large companies. The team includes individuals from psychology, computer science, engineering, management, and anthropology (me). This project is funded by an initiative from the National Science

Foundation (NSF), "Transformations to Quality Organizations," but supported by private organizations as well as the government. This innovative NSF program was at one time headed by NAPA "elder" Marietta Baba. I considered this research to be an example of the type of work a practicing anthropologist within an academic institution can conduct. **The companies that are the participants in this study are partners in the research and expect to gain practical insights into the working of teams.**

In my work with American Indians, I feel I bridge the gap between practice and traditional academia. I have participated in a consortium composed of four local American Indian organizations and the university. Our goal is to develop a culturally based substance abuse program for urban Indian adolescents that would include a youth summer camp at the university. I am currently assisting a traditional American Indian religious specialist in recording certain religious knowledge in danger of being lost. My strong feelings about the ethical responsibility anthropologists have to practice is a result of conversations with American Indian colleagues. Anthropologists have made careers of "studying" native communities without contributing anything to those communities in return. If we are going to show up in native communities and conduct our often rather esoteric and ethnocentric studies, we have a responsibility to also use our energy and influence to assist those communities in projects of their choosing.

I feel privileged to work in a position that allows me to bridge the gap between academia and practice. In a school of applied social science and a program of applied anthropology, the value and sophistication of practice are never questioned. Instead we hope to join with like-minded others as leaders in shaping the university of the future, where pure research and practice will be equally valued.

Originally appeared in Anthropology Newsletter, *April 1995*
Revised, spring 1998 and summer 1999

A Double Life in Anthropology

Eileen M. Mulhare
Colgate University

Eileen Mulhare, 1987

My vitae looks as if I have lived two lives in parallel. Perhaps I have. To my colleagues in Mesoamerican studies, I am an ethnologist and ethnohistorian who holds a research appointment at Colgate University. To my colleagues in the nonprofit sector, I am an applied anthropologist/management consultant doing business under the name of Institutional Advancement Services. **Academic anthropology is my passion, but applied anthropology pays the bills.** Fortunately, the education I received as an undergraduate anthropology major at Carlow College (1969–72) prepared me for both career tracks. My mother, medical anthropologist Mirta de la Torre Mulhare, designed Carlow's rigorous, five-field program to include an obligatory field placement. This was my first plunge into an alien culture: 250-plus hours of home visits to welfare recipients on behalf of a community mental health center. By the time I entered the doctoral program at the University of Pittsburgh, at the age of 19, I felt like a seasoned fieldworker. My "summer money" in graduate school came from working for nonprofit agencies as a field researcher and client advocate.

Nevertheless, I planned on a career in academia and considered applied anthropology as only a sideline. This squared with the program at Pitt in that era (1972–79), which emphasized four-field training coupled with overseas fieldwork. The collapse of the academic job market in late 1979, just as I was returning from two years of dissertation fieldwork in Totimehuacan (State of Puebla, Mexico), compelled me to rethink my options. By early 1981, after a string of glamorous but low-paid, temporary jobs in contract research and journalism, I was desperate for steady work.

I established myself in nonprofit management by starting "at the bottom," literally, as a receptionist for a home health service. The agency was computerizing its operations. **Anyone who was even vaguely computer literate, as I was then, received rapid promotions.** Within six months I was heading the patient accounts department, supervising a staff of 20, and earning more than an assistant professor. All told, from 1981 to 1990, I changed employers four times, moved from the East Coast to the

87

Midwest, switched from patient accounting to college fund-raising (another heavily computerized field), and rose to the level of director of development for an academic division of an urban research university.

Throughout those years, the generous salary and vacation time allowed me to continue doing fieldwork in Totimehuacan, for a few weeks at a stretch, at annual intervals. I wrote and defended my dissertation in 1986, while working 80-hour weeks directing the alumni section of a college's capital campaign.

In 1990, I returned to academia permanently as a research associate in anthropology at Colgate. **To make ends meet, I advise nonprofits in three areas of management: strategic planning, fund-raising programs, and office automation.** For example, in 1994–95, I had a one-year contract with the National Society of Fund Raising Executives (NSFRE) and a major foundation to help a minority nonprofit strengthen its fund-raising operations. The bulk of my practice involves conducting training seminars, often sponsored by NSFRE chapters in the United States or Canada.

I have written elsewhere about the applications of anthropology to nonprofit management (1984, 1992). A major inspiration for me has been the writings of the late James Spradley, the 1970s' foremost advocate of ethnography as a method for understanding complex society. **I see no difference, analytically or methodologically, between investigating the inner workings of a saint's cult in a Mexican village and analyzing the customary behavior of billing clerks in an American health care agency.** Both represent microcultures comprehensible to the outsider by means of participant-observation.

I grant that problem solving for paying clients takes more than good ethnography. Ingenuity, technical knowledge, and practical experience all play a role. But ethnography remains the foundation, revealing the patterns of beliefs and behaviors that contribute to a problem or can contribute to a culturally appropriate solution. It is this philosophy that makes whatever I do for a living "anthropological," no matter which side of my double life takes precedence at the moment.

References Cited

Mulhare, Eileen M.
  1984   Anthropology in Fund Raising Administration. Practicing Anthropology 6(1):13–14.
  1992   Projecting Anthropology to Nonprofit Managers. NAPA column. Anthropology Newsletter 33(5):17.

Originally appeared in Anthropology Newsletter, *March 1995*
Revised, spring 1998 and summer 1999

My Journey along the Path of Public Health

Myrna Silverman
University of Pittsburgh

Myrna Silverman

My career as an anthropologist in public health began 24 years ago, just after completing my doctoral work in cultural anthropology at the University of Pittsburgh. My dissertation research was on a local ethnic group in the Pittsburgh community. As it happened, I was approached by a fellow anthropologist to join a team of multidisciplinary researchers in the Graduate School of Public Health to provide assistance with the design and conduct of qualitative studies of 16 communities in the United States that were developing their emergency medical services systems. The opportunity to participate in a different type of traditional anthropological research appealed to me, and I joined the faculty of the Department of Health Services Administration at the University of Pittsburgh's Graduate School of Public Health and continued in this research career.

My career took a new direction as the field of gerontology grew and attracted anthropologists to its fold. I joined the Association of Anthropology and Gerontology, began teaching courses on health and aging, and developed a research portfolio on those topics. My early work concentrated on the evaluation of local programs and services for the aged and generally involved study of the process of program implementation. By the late 1980s, after discussions with colleagues in the field of geriatrics about a new type of health care assessment for older adults (Geriatric Assessment Units [GAUs]), I undertook a five-year study of the effectiveness of GAUs. It was my first research funded by the National Institutes of Health. **This research was designed as a randomized clinical trial. My training had not prepared me for this type of research. However, my prior experience of working with an interdisciplinary team enabled me to select a team of researchers with the appropriate skills to conduct the research.** This project, completed in 1994, was one of the major challenges of my research career and motivated me to develop the quantitative skills necessary to do this kind of research.

The project led to others, addressing questions that arose in the course of the work. Examples are, What are the barriers and facilitators to health care for older adults? How do these vary in different ethnic, racial, and income groups? What factors, such as economics, prior experience with the health care system, and social supports, affect how older adults take care of their health problems? Around that time, in addition to my faculty appointment, I was appointed **director of the Training and Information Core at the University of Pittsburgh's Alzheimer's Disease Research Center.** One of my responsibilities was to develop research evaluating the care of persons with Alzheimer's disease. I undertook an evaluation of a newly built residential Alzheimer's facility and, working with an interdisciplinary team, assessed the effects of this new model of care on the residents, their families, staff, and administration in that facility. Once again, the need for a skilled research team that could address these complex questions was required, as was the **need to combine traditional ethnographic research and structured quantitative measurements.**

The most recent research project (funded by the National Institute on Aging) explores the responses to **health care management of older African Americans and whites with chronic diseases.** Working with an interdisciplinary team of sociologists and anthropologists, we interviewed 768 older adults (half African American and half European American) in Allegheny County, Pennsylvania, and conducted follow-up interviews with a smaller group of these respondents over a two-year period, again combining qualitative and quantitative approaches. The purpose of the study was to learn how and why they combine the use of formal, informal, and self-care. We are in the process of extending this study to focus more on self-care and its role in health care management. Most recently I have been asked to conduct a qualitative study to learn the culture of family practice clinics and the barriers to immunology of older adults.

At the time I received my training, medical anthropology was in its infancy. Now programs in medical anthropology have become more common. I would say that my type of anthropology is a mix of applied, medical, and cultural anthropology. Generally, I select what I need from each of these fields to address the research questions. What I think makes me distinct from my colleagues in traditional anthropology is that I work with multidisciplinary teams of researchers. **Working in a school of public health that is closely allied to a medical school in a large university and with other universities in the area—where I can draw on the expertise of many disciplines—has been a luxury and has provided me with a rich and stimulating career in this field.** The increased numbers of anthropologists working at the School of Public Health (four in my department) imply that this is a promising environment for our colleagues. Whereas research takes up the majority of my work time, developing a teaching program in health and aging and directing the doctoral program for my department have provided me with a well-rounded career in public health.

Originally appeared in Anthropology Newsletter, *December 1995*
Revised, spring 1998 and summer 1999

Practicing Anthropology in Public Health and Medical Education

Sue Gena Lurie
Texas College of Osteopathic Medicine
and School of Public Health

Sue G. Lurie, Fort Worth, c. 1993

As an anthropologist and assistant professor in a university health science center, my professional role involves academic and applied teaching, participatory research and practice. Development of a new graduate program in public health has expanded these roles since my first practitioner profile in *Anthropology Newsletter* (in 1995) and the article on my work as a medical anthropologist in our College of Osteopathic Medicine (1992). I am about to complete my 12th year in this non-tenure-track position, now a joint one in the Department of Medical Humanities and the School of Public Health. **This combined role offers new opportunities in the context of national initiatives to integrate medicine and public health and the national "Healthy Communities" movement, with implications for local responsibility in health and social programs and development.** It also poses increasing challenges related to the competition among organizational and professional segments and community groups.

Sociocultural, medical, and practicing anthropology perspectives have been valuable in integrating these areas, as have my interests in organizations and professions. I plan health and medical career education projects, serve on diverse faculty and community committees, and am adviser for the Multicultural Medical Students Association. In medical humanities, I teach in the case-based, interdisciplinary medical ethics course, direct this course for physicians' assistant students, and serve on the hospital ethics committee and county medical ethics consortium. I also teach family and health, spirituality and health, and cross-cultural issues in patient care; and I coordinate community health agency observations and volunteer services in family medicine.

In the Master's in Public Health program, I teach community health and medical anthropology, and I collaborate in applied research and community assessment planning with public and private health and social agencies, ethnic leaders, and local residents. These projects include community monitoring, using qualitative methods in a national substance abuse program for youth, neighborhood needs assessment and community mobilization for health, evaluation of a domestic violence health education intervention project, compiling an interagency data bank on substance abuse information, ethnographic research on health needs of African American elderly residents, and surveys of Hispanic family and minority adolescents' health needs and service utilization. **Practicing anthropology is the implicit basis of my roles** as liaison or board member in a variety of health, mental health, and social service agencies and coalitions for youth, the elderly, the homeless, and diabetes education/intervention.

While my identity as an anthropologist has been grounded through adjunct teaching at the University of North Texas in psychological and medical anthropology, the anthropology of work, and the Far East—the site of my dissertation research on the professionalization of nursing and community health (Hong Kong), **my major professional roles are in the health sciences.** This followed a ten-year career in teaching anthropology over two periods of graduate school—at the University of North Carolina (M.A.) and University of Oklahoma (Ph.D.) and a National Institute of Mental Health postdoctoral fellowship in ethnography and public policy at Northwestern University. My applied positions have included research in maternal and child health at the University of North Carolina School of Public Health, in-service education at Oklahoma Children's Hospital, curriculum coordination for physicians' assistants at the University of Texas Southwestern Medical Center, and General Educational Development, or GED, teaching for inner-city youth in Dallas.

My broad training in the theory and four fields of anthropology has led to my own professional "evolution" in interdisciplinary and participatory research and practice. **The close relationship of practice to theory and research is continually challenged, and often confirmed, by collaboration with health and medical professionals, community members, and groups that are changing their own roles from informants or subjects to colleagues.** The anthropological imperatives of understanding and respecting our own and others' perspectives and their ethical integration in the development of social policy and programs are no less significant in contemporary society than in the last decade. These imperatives will become even more essential in the next decade. With the new millennium, we need to keep our focus and reflect on our unique practice.

Reference Cited

Lurie, Sue Gena
    1992   Medical Anthropologist at Work. Anthropology Newsletter 13(6) September: 16.

Originally appeared in Anthropology Newsletter, *January 1995*
Revised, spring 1998 and summer 1999

Constructing a Workplace: A Personal Tale from a Practicing Anthropologist

Elaine Simon
University of Pennsylvania

It is always easier to find coherence after the fact than to plan a coherent life, and so it is in making sense of a career. I could say that I planned to be a practicing anthropologist and deliberately worked toward my current lofty status, but I would be fantasizing. To begin with, there are no models. All of us who do this work have had to invent it and ourselves in the process. In my case, **I have followed my interests, taken advantage of opportunities, made some compromises, and eventually constructed a workplace both inside and outside of an academic institution.**

I have worked in many different settings that have drawn on my anthropological thinking. After completing a master's degree in urban education and a two-year stint as a high school teacher, I returned to school to study anthropology with the hope of gaining insight into the culture of schools and bureaucratic organizations, as well as into the urban setting and diverse populations I encountered. During my graduate student period, I also had a number of opportunities to apply my anthropological thinking and research skills in contract research firms and research divisions of public agencies. I evaluated education and adult employment and training programs and developed community profiles. After I finished my Ph.D. in 1983, I did more consulting and then assumed a visiting professorship in urban studies at Temple University (where I had studied for my Ph.D.). **Now at the University of Pennsylvania, I continue to do educational evaluation and research with a nonprofit research organization and codirect the graduate and undergraduate programs in urban studies.**

As a practicing anthropologist, I have constructed a workplace that meets my needs. I am someone who appreciates theory, but **my talents and tendencies have led me to want to make practical applications of theory.** I have shaped my career out of choices that reflect my need to participate in conversations that come from both theoretical and practical perspectives. **In a sense, the career I chronicle here is a construction, still in progress.**

I am now codirector of the urban studies program (for more details, see http://www.sas.upenn.edu/urban/) at the University of Pennsylvania. I work with both undergraduates, teaching a research seminar and overseeing their internships, and graduate students in the Urban Studies Graduate Certificate Program. I also do qualitative evaluation and research on education reform and community revitalization. My interests are in participatory research and in the connection of schools and communities. I teach a graduate course in the School of Education on qualitative evaluation with my colleague and long-time friend Jolley Christman. Jolley started the nonprofit research firm called Research for Action a few years ago, and much of the research I am involved in is as an associate of that organization. I have a great deal of flexibility in my daily schedule, which allows me to fulfill obligations both at Penn and at Research for Action. It does not, however, leave much room for academic writing, which I regret.

In the university part of my workplace, I feel constantly challenged to push the limits of the questions I ask—to look at my work in a larger context. This stimulation informs my continuing educational evaluation research. I also learn a great deal from my students, and I think that they appreciate a teacher who is doing applied work and research in the world.

At Research for Action I am connected to people struggling to improve the chances of kids and to help organizations become more reflective about their work. **Research for Action is different from other "contract" research firms I have worked for because the associates self-consciously take a stance on the kind of work they do and how they work together.** It is an organization dedicated to participatory research and issues of social justice. As a workplace, Research for Action tries to understand itself as a feminist organization, which forces colleagues to consider assumptions underlying methodology and relationships.

When I decided to get a Ph.D., I did not deliberately intend to pursue a traditional academic path. I had some pressing questions I wanted to explore, and that was about as concrete a goal as I had. I soon found myself working in contract research settings as an anthropologist, which seemed incredibly lucky in some ways. But there was something unsatisfying about working in those settings. While I learned a lot about policy and writing for nonacademic audiences during that period, I felt constrained both politically and intellectually. I feel that my current constructed workplace, hectic as it is, satisfies my need to answer questions that matter to people in education, as well as my need to think about those questions in the broad context of changing urban economic, social, and spatial conditions. Though I retain the outlook, the methodological orientation, and the appreciation of complexity of the anthropologist, the literature I read ranges across disciplines.

My constructed workplace allows me to teach, work with students to find their own niches, carry out research on topics I care very much about, and interact with colleagues who force my constant intellectual renewal. **Another aspect of my constructed workplace is its location only four blocks from my home—giving me an old-fashioned urban existence. That was the one thing I actually planned from the beginning.**

Originally appeared in Anthropology Newsletter, *May 1994*
Revised, spring 1998 and summer 1999

Integrating Anthropologists into Nonacademic Work Settings

Cris Johnsrud
Southern Technology Applications Center

A friend and I have a long-running argument about whether or not he is really an anthropologist. We were both graduate students in anthropology at the same institution, and after earning our degrees, he took a position in community college administration while I became associated with a regional technology transfer center headquartered at a university. **Although we were both associated with academic institutions, he did not view himself as an anthropologist or feel that what he was doing involved anthropology. I, on the other hand, have always felt myself to be an anthropologist, despite the fact that I do not teach, am not associated with an anthropology department, and am principally involved with program design and development, management, and strategic planning.**

The image of what anthropology is and what anthropologists do is central to many of the issues facing the discipline as growing numbers of graduates seek employment in nonacademic settings. **Creating and maintaining a strong "market niche" outside academe are critical if anthropology is to have a recognizable, sustained, and positive impact on local, national, and global issues and programs.** Yet, like my friend, there are many successful professional individuals with both undergraduate and graduate degrees in anthropology who do not consider themselves to be anthropologists and, perhaps most important, who do not recognize or acknowledge the contributions of the anthropological training, perspectives, and approaches to their successes. How, then, is anthropology to become recognized by outside employers as an important and valuable organizational asset? **How can anthropologists create, expand, and strengthen anthropology's presence outside the academy?**

Significantly, **the barriers encountered by the anthropology community in attempts to build a substantial and sizable presence outside the academy are largely the result of the organizational and structural characteristics of anthropology inside the academy.** The values, expectations, rewards and incentives, and career development mechanisms that make for successful careers inside the academy are in many cases maladaptive outside it. This is not to criticize academic anthropology. We teach what we know. Unfortunately, what we know is often insufficient for nonacademic career development.

Several elements are necessary for integrating anthropologists and anthropology much more strongly into nonacademic settings: (1) network development, (2) participant-observation and entrepreneurship, (3) "market" research, and (4) endorsement of anthropologists within the academy. These elements have been identified during the past several years from my own experiences as a practicing anthropologist who works with engineers and business professionals and supervises anthropology and engineering students working on funding projects.

Network Development

A primary strategy for integrating anthropology and anthropologists into nonacademic sectors is the development of networks outside anthropology and outside the academy. This can create opportunities for employment of anthropology graduates and help faculty members identify new research and funding opportunities. Encouraging anthropology students to attend conferences and other special events organized by and for nonanthropological professional groups helps them identify potential career development arenas and establish such networks. These events provide preliminary views of the field of career interest, yield important insights into areas in which anthropological perspectives are absent but needed, serve as an introduction to the cultural attributes (language, dress, behavior, social organization, power hierarchies, etc.) of the area of interest, and provide opportunities for developing professional networks for career development. Additionally, they provide anthropology with visibility and a "presence" outside the academy.

Participant-Observation and Entrepreneurship

One of the most powerful tools acquired by anthropologists is the ability to organize research using ethnographic methods. It provides practitioners with a way to understand events and contexts, identify opportunities, develop ways to become involved in those opportunities, and illustrate the value of anthropological contributions to potential employers. **Participant-observation flavored with what might be called "entrepreneurship" can help establish rewarding careers.** That is, in order to apply anthropological knowledge and perspective to solving or helping to solve a particular problem, practitioners can utilize participant-observation and conduct various levels of fieldwork to learn as much as possible about the problem, the actors (both individual and organizational), the context, program goals, and potential outcomes/impacts. Further, this knowledge is useful in identifying opportunities for career development as an employee or as an external consultant.

Most practitioners today must be extremely entrepreneurial in developing practitioner careers. This requires several skills, including an appropriate degree of assertiveness, excellent fieldwork skills to interpret organizational contexts and recognize opportunities when they arise, the ability to communicate in nonanthropological terms, tenacity, and the ability to project an image, especially in the private sector, of willingness to learn. **Indeed, it may be the last skill that is the most important for those wishing to establish practitioner careers in business and industry.**

How can students acquire these skills? There are no easy answers, for some of these skills are inherent in the personality of the would-be practitioner. Despite this, course work that includes presentations from practitioners, role playing, case studies, and simulations of anthropological involvement in nonacademic scenarios can provide students with some appreciation of what they will face outside the academy. Alternatively, there are several resources available through college and university career resource centers and through privately offered seminars, although the latter tend to have price tags that are beyond the means of many students.

"Market" Research

Establishing a nonacademic market for anthropology graduates is extremely problematic, and the primary activity has been to rely on the entrepreneurial efforts of individual anthropologists who, through their own ingenuity and diligence, have forged a path that others can follow into government and/or industry career settings. This has reinforced the need for network development among practitioners with significant assistance from NAPA, local practitioner organizations, and other formal and informal organizations. Despite these efforts, this process is still slow and haphazard. Serendipity plays as much a part in the formation of a practitioner career as do networks and training. Most practitioners stumble on opportunities, and many other opportunities go unrecognized.

In contrast to cultural anthropology, **other professions utilize different approaches to developing employment opportunities for their graduates.** It may be useful to study these different approaches for applicability to anthropology departments. For example, the College of Engineering at the University of Florida utilizes strategies at both the individual faculty level and the department and college levels to assist engineering graduates to find employment. Close watch is kept on hiring trends, emerging opportunities, and comparisons of employment rates of the university's engineering graduates with those of other colleges and universities. Also, external industry advisory boards provide additional insights into emerging employment needs.

Whether or not such measures could be effective for departments of anthropology is a matter that requires considerable scrutiny. However, **for such measures to be implemented on a wide scale within anthropology, there must be endorsement by the anthropological community within the academy.** It is to that consideration that I now turn.

For anthropology students who wish to be practitioners, a number of skills must be taught along with the established curriculum. Much of anthropological training stresses critique, and this is one of the major strengths of the discipline. Yet this by itself is insufficient to those seeking to develop practitioner careers outside the academy. This is because a prevailing attitude outside the academy is, "Don't be part of the problem; be part of the solution." **The ability to provide critical thinking is essential in industry and government, so that problems are understood. However, without the concomitant skill of suggesting ways to "fix it" (which implies taking risks and making decisions), critique alone is inadequate.** Simply pointing out flaws in arguments, program designs, and other decisions leads to a perception that the anthropologist is just another critic. Negativity is not tolerated for long in industry or government settings.

Another essential skill is the ability to work in teams, a capability that cannot be overemphasized. Working in applied settings is about teamwork, and anthropologists are often at a significant disadvantage in this regard. Teaming is difficult yet necessary. **Teamwork must be integrated into curricular activities at both the graduate and the undergraduate levels, even though the concept is generally not part of the cultural anthropological ethos.**

Third, **anthropology students must learn to meet deadlines.** Missing the window effectively silences the anthropologist's contributions to important issues and maintains the marginality of the discipline in the eyes of power holders and decision makers in all sectors of society, including the university.

Conclusion

Anthropology is just now beginning to address in an organized manner the issues of creating a strong, viable "market" for graduates outside the academy. The absence of existing external niches for anthropology graduates, training that can help students acquire needed job-related skills, public understanding of what anthropology is and what anthropologists can do, and networks that span academic, private, and government sectors must be addressed immediately if anthropology is to grow rather than fade into obscurity as interesting but irrelevant.

Note

Editor's note: This article is excerpted from a longer essay of the same name published in *Transforming Academia: Challenges and Opportunities for an Engaged Anthropology,* edited by Linda Basch, Lucie Wood Saunders, Jagna Wojcicka Sharff, and James Peacock (American Ethnological Society Monograph, 8, Arlington, VA: American Anthropological Association, 1999).

Originally appeared in Anthropology Newsletter, *March 1997*
Revised, spring 1998 and summer 1999

Directing Organizational Culture Change through Strategic Planning and Leadership

Dennis Wiedman

Dennis Wiedman
Florida International University

If one views anthropology as the study of humans in all their complexities throughout time and in all places, then anthropological theories and methods should be replicable and useful in any human situation, not only among exotic and distant peoples but in our own society and institutions as well. Currently my activities in practicing anthropology focus on organizational culture and directed culture change. Since 1990 I have served as assistant to the provost at Florida International University (FIU), one of ten public universities in Florida. Using anthropological perspectives, I **facilitate planning, accreditation, and policy development for the university, which primarily serves the culturally diverse 3.5 million people of South Florida.** FIU ranks fourth among U.S. universities in the number of bachelor's degrees awarded to minority students, and more than half of the faculty are minorities and/or women. Since 1988 FIU rapidly developed from 17,500 to 32,000 students and more than doubled the number of doctoral degree programs to 24.

How this organization managed growth while adjusting for state budget cuts and the impact of Hurricane Andrew has provided a natural laboratory for anthropological research. Also, during this time, accrediting agencies mandated the implementation of ongoing planning and evaluation, and the state legislature called for increased accountability with goals and measurable outcomes. Changes in organizational culture are noticeable in the transition from present to future thinking, from crisis management to strategic planning, and from oral to written traditions (Wiedman 1992).

Accreditation and state legislature demands resulted in the formulation and writing of plans, goals, measurable outcomes, policies, and procedures. Such practices **force academic subcultures to develop written traditions, thus making explicit what was implicit when orally communicated.** In the development of written policies and plans, ethnographic skills are invaluable in documenting behaviors, beliefs, and practices. The understanding of social structure, social organization, and culture change facilitates the building of a consensus for setting priorities concerning goals and policies. And the understanding of linguistic and cognitive processes allows for the creation of words and symbols to portray a future vision built on acceptable cultural themes.

Over the past decade, American businesses, organizations, and institutions have undergone similar transitions to increase productivity and efficiency through "strategic planning" and other initiatives. These could be viewed as management fads; however, they could also be seen as sociocultural adaptations to a changing environment. They come at a time in human evolution when **the invention and diffusion of electronic information technology are revolutionizing the communication patterns, decision making, and authority structures of the workplace and organizations.** Strategic planning is a conscious, purposeful effort to influence the future. To be successful at these efforts, one must consider the organization's external environment, especially the political, economic, and demographic influences. The anthropological perspective considers these macroinfluences as well as the microprocesses of human interactions and beliefs. From a comparative analysis of organizations implementing strategic planning, I have identified recurrent patterns of organizational culture change. Based on this knowledge, there are numerous roles that anthropologists can take to influence the strategic planning process (Wiedman 1998).

From the organizational culture perspective, the university consists of subsets of individuals interacting in networks of communication and exchanges which exhibit distinguishing traits. Cultural manifestations, thus, are elaborated as members interact to confront similar problems and, in attempting to cope with them, devise and employ strategies to be passed on to new members. These can be viewed as subcultures, each with its own cognitive paradigm, language categories, dress codes, expected behaviors, and so on. Considering this context, **my role has been to organize information, symbols, and people in ways that influence the allocation of resources and facilitate change in directions consistent with the goal of the university**—to be recognized as a top, public, urban, research university. More strategically, working with the president and vice presidents and facilitating broad-base discussion over many years, the university identified five academic themes and two management philosophies in which to excel and focus resources. Since 1996 the academic themes of "international," "urban," "environment," "health," and "information" have guided the development of academic teaching, research, and service; the management philosophies of "quality" and "diversity" guide the ways in which administrative units strive to excel.

What training and experiences prepared me for this role? An **education in the four subfields of anthropology is my foundation,** for it provides the broad, holistic perspective that distinguishes anthropology from other social sciences and allows for a diversity of explanations and methods to complement interdisciplinary endeavors. My training began with a high school anthropology class here in Miami. While studying for a bachelor's degree in anthropology at the University of Florida, I learned from Charles Fairbanks the importance of ethnohistory and the influence of the past on the present (Wiedman 1988). Brian Du Toit taught me how the revitalization process is recurrent among humans everywhere. But **it was not until I experienced several years of traditional participant-observation among Native Americans in Oklahoma that I recognized the importance of applied anthropology.**

While learning the intricacies of Peyotism as practiced in northeast Oklahoma, I realized that the Native American Church should be viewed not only as a religion but also as a health care delivery system that complements biomedical systems (Wiedman 1990). I realized that if I gain knowledge from Native Americans, I should attempt to give something in return. Working on this premise, I chose to study the leading Native American health problem, diabetes mellitus, a disease unknown among them prior to 1940. This resulted in my 1979 doctoral dissertation at the University of Oklahoma and my subsequent contributions to understanding diabetes throughout the world, especially as populations acculturate to industrialized economies and lifestyles (Wiedman 1989).

Although my graduate training at the University of Oklahoma followed the four-field approach, an important role model was Morris Opler, who, as an early applied anthropologist worked with Japanese Americans detained in California internment camps during World War II. I gained an ecological perspective from Stephen Thompson and a perspective on the cross-cultural analysis of elites from Joseph Whitecotton. Also, I assisted Robert Hill in an interdisciplinary study of psychosocial stress and injuries in the Oklahoma City Fire Department. This experience introduced surveys, computers, and quantitative analysis into my study of urban institutions.

In 1980, my wife and I returned to Miami in order to begin our family among our own kin. I began teaching as an adjunct instructor at FIU, and with the leadership of Hazel Weidman, I joined the Office of Transcultural Education and Research in the Department of Psychiatry at the University of Miami School of Medicine. I was a unit director of a geriatrics community mental health unit in a local neighborhood. This position followed from **Hazel Weidman's "Miami Health Ecology Project," in which she envisioned the anthropologist as a culture broker between an ethnic group and the biomedical system.** This experience in clinically applied anthropology not only provided management experience but also impressed on me how anthropologists could direct culture change (Wiedman 1984).

After years with adjunct status at the two schools, I decided to establish a corporation to provide social science research to community agencies and businesses. For example, a two-year project included evaluations of kindergarten through high school educational programs for

Haitians in the Dade County schools. In addition to teaching at FIU, I led several multidisciplinary grant-writing efforts to support the establishment of the Southeast Florida Center on Aging.

My ability to coordinate groups of faculty was recognized in 1988 when **FIU asked me to become associate director of the university's reaffirmation of accreditation by the Southern Association of Colleges and Schools (SACS).** This entailed a two-year self-study of every unit in the university and the mobilization of practically every member of the faculty and staff. SACS had recently changed the accreditation criteria to include institutional effectiveness, and few schools had conducted self-studies under this new requirement, which called for ongoing planning and evaluation. I viewed it as an opportunity to direct culture change. SACS recognized the FIU self-study as the best by a large public university that year and asked me to present the FIU model at its annual meeting, where I found myself speaking to more than 300 college presidents and self-study directors. **Since 1990, I have continued to facilitate the planning process leading to the development of the university's strategic plan, which details the direction of the university into the 21st century** (Wiedman 1996).

To enhance my professional skills, I was trained by the National Center for Higher Education Management Systems to link strategic planning, budgets, and information systems. In this role of strategic planning for the university, my skills in quantitative and qualitative data analysis, experience with the computerization and management of vast amounts of information, and ability to identify historical trends as the basis for future forecasts were of utmost importance.

Over the past two years I have taken on the new role of academic affairs Web master, enhancing the wide distribution and discussion of plans, policies, and organizational information. What was once only on paper or verbally communicated is now available to the entire university community. Overall, my role has been to organize information, symbols, and people in ways that influence the allocation of resources and facilitate change in directions consistent with the goals of the university. An example of this is the strategically identified management philosophy of "diversity," which over the years has stimulated special programs, campus activities, and employee training. In 1998 an external consultant conducting student opinion surveys showed that ethnicity and racial issues are not major factors for students withdrawing from school. Considering that FIU has grown so rapidly in the past ten years, and that it has one of the most diverse student bodies and faculties in the United States, ethnic and racial conflicts are minimal (Wiedman 1999).

These strategic planning and leadership skills enabled me—in a desire to contribute to the anthropological profession—to better serve as treasurer of the Society for Applied Anthropology from 1996 to 1999. In this role I linked budget requests directly to the society's goals, enabling the board of directors to make more informed decisions regarding the initiatives supported with their resources.

Applied anthropologists continue to face a double bind. As noted by Hazel Weidman (1976), we produce research that develops new programs, but frequently we do not receive authority to manage them. Pursuing this challenge and given the insights gained from our cross-cultural and holistic paradigm, if applied anthropologists want to make a significant difference, we must create new policy- and decision-making roles that can influence cultural change. **Practicing anthropologists should be trained to seek leadership roles and the authority to implement what anthropological research produces.**

Seldom do anthropologists gain access to elites with authority, and when they earn the position, they rarely publish their experiences. Similarities and differences exist among every group, so anthropological theories should apply no matter where people are. **It is important that applied/practicing anthropologists publish their experiences in order to refine and advance our understanding of humanity and, just as important, how anthropology can address human problems and critical social issues.**

References Cited

Weidman, Hazel Hitson
   1976   In Praise of the Double Bind Inherent in Anthropological Application. *In* Do Applied Anthropologists Apply Anthropology? Michael Angrosino, ed. Pp. 105–117. Athens: University of Georgia Press.
Wiedman, Dennis
   1984   Directing Geriatric Health Care: Some Practical Issues. Practicing Anthropology 6(3):7–8.
   1988   Ethnohistory: A Researcher's Guide. Studies in Third World Societies, 35. Williamsburg, VA: Studies in Third World Societies.
   1989   Adiposity or Longevity: Which Factor Accounts for the Increase of Type II Diabetes Mellitus When Populations Acculturate to an Industrial Technology? Medical Anthropology 11(3):237–252.
   1990   Big and Little Moon Peyotism as Health Care Delivery Systems. Medical Anthropology 12(4):371–387.
   1992   Effects on Academic Culture of Shifts from Oral to Written Traditions: The Case of University Accreditation. Human Organization 51(4):398–407.
   1996   Florida International University: Reaching for the Top. 2nd edition. University Strategic Plan, December 20. Dennis Wiedman, comp. and ed. Miami: Florida International University.
   1998   Effective Strategic Planning Roles for Anthropologists. Practicing Anthropology 20:136–139.
   1999   Celebrating Diversity at FIU: A Role Model for the Future of U.S. Higher Education. Diversity in Education, special issue. Journal for the Art of Teaching 6(1):37–46.

Originally appeared in Anthropology Newsletter, *December 1994*
Revised, September 1999

Uniting Theory and Practice in American Corporations

Marietta Baba
Wayne State University

As an anthropologist practicing in industry, I am doing the most exciting work of my career. Today, my students and I are working inside several major corporations to better understand the interaction of strategic change initiatives and sociocultural context and to influence change processes in ways that enhance the participation of working people. Some examples of the kind of work we do include

- collaborating with a global group of anthropologists to form the first-ever advisory board of anthropologists for Motorola—an effort that is intended to stimulate anthropological research on the social context of advanced technologies in emerging markets around the globe;
- ethnohistorical fieldwork in European and American business units of a major consumer products corporation, focused on capturing employee points of view on major organizational change, including mergers and acquisitions, open office architecture, category management, and a number of other types of change; and
- qualitative and quantitative simulation modeling of the dynamics of cross-functional teamwork at Ford Motor Company, with an emphasis on understanding factors, such as power balance and trust between management and employees, that influence team performance.

What all of these projects have in common is the **creative reformulation of classical anthropological concepts and methods for understanding human experience that is on the cutting-edge of global change.** The changes we are witnessing will define the world of the 21st century. These include the rise of new and emerging markets, the transformation of corporate structures, and the ways in which human practices both shape and are influenced by these profound economic and organizational realignments.

Practitioners—those whose research is driven both by a problem orientation and theoretical questions—are generally the only anthropologists who have ready access to sites such as those noted above. Getting access to cutting-edge action in global business and industry requires that the anthropologist understand the current problems and issues of these organizations from their point of view and gain new understandings that contribute to the amelioration of their problems. The ability to conceptualize these problems theoretically and to extend theory through problem-oriented research enables us to advance both sound and innovative solutions on the one hand and contribute to the advancement of knowledge on the other hand. We are committed fully to both of these goals.

The hallmarks of our approach include (1) an extended period of fieldwork during which we go into the company or organization to learn about work group practices firsthand (i.e., from group members), (2) direct observation of work practices, (3) participant-observation of work process redesign teams, (4) emic conceptualizations of work processes and corporate change initiatives, (5) ethnographically based descriptions of the unique cultures of work groups and corporations and the role of these cultures in the change process, (6) validation of these descriptions and concepts with work groups members, and (7) development of tools and interventions that enable work groups to learn about their own work cultures and to introduce new technologies in ways that preserve and enhance work group learning. Companies value this approach because it reveals a critical dimension of the organization that they often have no other means of accessing. Members of work groups also view our approach favorably because it provides them with a stronger voice in the corporation and encourages their representation and participation in decision-making bodies (i.e., as an outcome of our interventions).

My training for this work was nontraditional, in the sense that I did not receive my doctoral degree in either cultural or applied anthropology. Rather, I was trained initially as a physical anthropologist and spent ten years working with Morris Goodman in the field of molecular evolution. Before that, I spent time at Yerkes Regional Primate Center in Georgia observing the threat gestures of gelada baboons. Both of these experiences were invaluable, although not in ways I expected at the time.

In Morris Goodman's lab I learned the ropes of the traditional Western scientific method (what some would call positivism), including how to construct a theoretically grounded research design, how to develop measures, how to analyze data using computer algorithms, how to interpret results and display data graphically, and how to write articles and publish. **I also learned the creative side of science—to spot anomalies, generate new constructs, develop alternative explanations. Understanding and being able to apply the philosophies and methodologies of science are invaluable when working in corporations and with other disciplines, for they enhance our legitimacy, permit anthropologists to communicate with others, and enable us to write proposals that get funded.** At the same time, the work at Yerkes proved to me the value of the naturalist's approach, including direct observation and the close description and recording of behavior. **The skills of the primate ethnologist thus provided me with a foundation for the later study of work behavior and culture in industry** (together with an intensive, self-directed retraining program that included exhaustive reading in the theory and methods of cultural anthropology, the anthropology of work, and the organizational and management sciences). I also earned an MBA degree (which, to me, was the rough equivalent of learning the native language).

Besides my research and practice in industry, I am a professor of anthropology, and I spend about one-half of my time teaching and advising approximately one dozen graduate students, many of whom relocated to the Detroit area from other states to study business and industry in our anthropology department. **I value my academic affiliation, and I am fortunate to work with an excellent group of graduate students. I do not view myself, however, as a traditional academic in an ivory tower. Rather, I see myself as an academic-industrial boundary spanner, who—together with colleagues from other disciplines—is trying to both develop and apply the theories and methods of anthropology and other social sciences to address some of our nation's most urgent economic problems.**

Although I have devoted my career to transferring anthropological knowledge to industry, I do not believe that anthropology alone can bring the kind of understanding needed to solve modern problems. Other disciplines have a great deal to teach anthropologists about the modern world; some of the most exciting discoveries made by our team have come as a result of team-based, multidisciplinary problem solving. Anthropologists and those in other sciences—much like the various disciplines and functions in industry—need to tear down the walls to collaboration and cooperation between us if we are to truly understand the world in which we live.

Originally appeared in Anthropology Newsletter, *September 1994*
Revised, spring 1998 and summer 1999

On Being an Anthropologist-Citizen

Rebecca M. Joseph
National Park Service

There are certain experiences that stay with one long after they have occurred, often acquiring significance far beyond the meaning attributed at the time. The annual Memorial Day Parade was a major civic event in the New York City suburb where I grew up. In 1972, the town was divided over the Vietnam War. Denied a place in the official parade, People for Peace obtained a permit to march behind it. Through taunts and jeers from a handful of bystanders, we had just started walking from City Hall when a man deliberately drove a large, white car into the procession. The driver was a veteran, a member of the local post of the American Legion. I was one of several kids up front carrying the group's banner who got hit. My family celebrated a special triumph at the Albert Leonard Junior High School graduation two years later when I received the American Legion Award for exemplary citizenship. The medal is still with me in a box of treasures safe on a high shelf in the bedroom closet.

As ethnography program manager for the northeast region of the National Park Service, **I engage with the ironies, agonies, triumphs, and ambiguities of the national narrative every day.** My work focuses on brokering information among anthropologists, people with distinctive connections to national parks, federal managers, and field staff to support and expand culturally informed decision making and productive collaborations. What I like most about my job is the opportunities it affords to join scholarship and praxis at many levels and in varying contexts. The research and intervention projects that I develop and manage are diverse. Some are very broad in scope, such as a study of relationships between African Americans and national park resources in four states and the regional implementation of the Native American Graves Protection and Repatriation Act (NAGPRA). Others are site specific and meet strategic management needs, including an evaluation of the oral history program at Ellis Island, ethnographic documentation of farming practices in and around Lexington-Concord, Massachusetts, and assessments of cultural resources such as a Cape Cod cranberry bog for possible nomination to the National Register of Historic Places as traditional cultural properties.

One of my favorite projects involved the largest community garden in the United States. The site at Floyd Bennett Field in Brooklyn is on New York City's first commercial airfield, now a part of Gateway

National Recreation Area. Involving the work of anthropologists Steven Parish and Rita Shakya and a group of management students, the project documented how the garden is formally and informally organized, as well as its social, cultural, and economic values to the gardeners and the park. The East New York Urban Youth Corps, a local community-based organization, was then enlisted to assist the gardeners in organizing a nonprofit organization and facilitate an agreement that transferred responsibility for ongoing operations from the government to the people with the greatest stake in the program, the newly formed Gateway Gardeners Association. In the first year alone, it saved the park more than $50,000, which was reallocated to meet critical needs and produced a host of new partnerships with, among others, the Brooklyn Botanical Garden.

Like many of my professional colleagues, **I view service to the field as an obligation as well as a means of staying connected to the broader discipline of anthropology. As program chair, I chose "Scholars and Activists" as the theme for the Society for Applied Anthropology's 1998 Annual Meeting in San Juan, Puerto Rico.** Working with an international program committee and six cosponsors (Association of Latina and Latino Anthropologists, Committee on Refugees and Immigrants, Political Ecology Society, Sun Coast Organization of Practicing Anthropologists, University of Puerto Rico, Puerto Rico Humanities Foundation–National Endowment for the Humanities), we attracted **1,000 participants from more than 30 countries to nearly 200 events and activities.** Key sessions included "The Languages of Puerto Rican Identity: A Dialogue between Writers and Anthropologists" and "Human Rights, Power, and Difference: Expanding Contemporary Interpretations of Human Rights in Theory and Practice." Serving as program chair gave me an opportunity to return to my colleagues, and the discipline, some of the support and energy that have furthered my professional development.

One area of anthropological practice that is of ongoing interest to me is ethics. **Professional ethics can and should be taught as integral components of all undergraduate- and graduate-level anthropology courses.** Ethical guidelines developed by the American Anthropological Association (AAA) and other professional organizations should be widely distributed and adhered to. Still, we must recognize that no code of professional ethics, training, or threat of sanctions, including exclusion from the peer community, can transform or even be expected to always integrate well with the moral codes that individual anthropologists bring to their work. Applied anthropologists, especially practitioners, work at the frontiers of anthropological ethics. Many of today's most prevalent issues were rare or nonexistent a decade ago. **During my tenure as the AAA *Anthropology Newsletter* ethics editor, the bimonthly feature has focused on interpreting and using the ethics code in emerging functional areas such as expert testimony and in locales, including much of Europe, with different standards and approaches to ethical concerns.**

I am often asked by students (and sometimes their parents) what kinds of paid work anthropologists do. Actually, they do a lot of things—as my career to date demonstrates. Before joining the National Park Service, I worked for several years at the Institute for Community Research, a non-profit research and community education organization in Hartford, Connecticut, where I established and managed two arts programs. The Cultural Heritage Arts Program is Connecticut's traditional and folks arts program, initially funded by the National Endowment for Arts as part of its effort to support statewide programs throughout the country. Its focus is on identifying, documenting, presenting, and publicizing the cultural traditions of Connecticut's diverse populations. The Urban Artists Initiative (formerly the Inner City Cultural Development Program), a partnership with the Connecticut Commission on the Arts, provides professional development assistance including training, mentors, and grants to artists and community-based organizations in Connecticut's major cities lacking access to mainstream sources of support.

My postgraduate career began at California State University at Long Beach, where **I was a founder of the applied anthropology program, the first master's level program in the West at an urban university.** Though I moved from an academic position to full-time practice in 1990, my involvement in students' professional development remains strong. Whenever funding is available, I offer paid traineeships that provide opportunities for graduate students in anthropology and related disciplines to experience working for land-managing agencies for periods ranging from ten weeks to one year. Past trainees have conducted ethnographic needs assessments and created NAGPRA inventories, among other projects. I am also a NAPA mentor.

Being an applied anthropologist offers many opportunities to participate in interdisciplinary teams and joint ventures. As a practitioner or professional anthropologist, this is the most common way for objectives to be accomplished, which is perfect for a curious person with broad interests and boundary-crossing inclinations. One of my more humorous anecdotes involves a contract research/intervention project, surgical scrubs, a pin saying "Dr. R. Joseph," and an orderly who needed an emergency room physician at 3:00 a.m.

Notably, **I did not know that there was a field called "applied anthropology" until I had completed my dissertation research and began to look for a full-time job.** As an undergraduate at Swarthmore College, I majored in sociology and anthropology after deciding that comparative religion and international relations were too focused on texts and elites, respectively, for my tastes. I cannot honestly say that I would have chosen an applied anthropology graduate program over a traditional one had I known of any at the time. **The doctoral program at the University of California at San Diego did not encourage applied work but did provide a solid theoretical and methodological grounding for my future professional**

development. Not surprisingly, I was drawn to Southeast Asia, where I eventually spent three years studying women artisans, government, and donor agency interventions in Indonesia.

I have always been a problem solver with a talent for finding value and hope in all kinds of people and places. I am proud of the work that I do and look forward to future opportunities to put my training and experience to further good use. As I am a 1999–2000 participant in the federal government's Executive Potential Program, my chance may well be just around the corner. The box of treasures goes with me.

Originally appeared in Anthropology Newsletter, *October 1995*
Revised, spring 1998 and summer 1999

Anthropology in Disaster Research and Management

Anthony Oliver-Smith
University of Florida

Background

In 1972, after receiving an M.A. in Latin American studies (1967) and while completing a Ph.D. in social anthropology from Indiana University (1974), I joined the faculty of the University of Florida. I am also a member of the International Research and Advisory Panel on the Study of Refugees and Other Displaced Persons at Oxford University. In 1996 I became a NAPA board member at large. I also currently serve on the executive board of the Society for Applied Anthropology. Previously, I worked as a field investigator for the Massachusetts Commission against Discrimination (1969, 1971) and as a field representative for the Peru Earthquake Relief Committee (1970). I have conducted fieldwork and consulted in a wide array of countries, including Peru, Spain, Honduras, Brazil, India, the United States, and Jamaica, on disaster management, displaced populations, and resettlement.

I feel as though **my greatest professional accomplishment is the publication of the only longitudinal ethnographic study of a natural disaster in the developing world, *The Martyred City: Death and Rebirth in the Andes*** (Oliver-Smith 1992).

Disaster Work

My work in disasters is somewhat misunderstood. When there is a disaster, I am frequently asked if I am going off to work on the emergency situation. This misconception of what I actually do in disaster work is often based on a misunderstanding of disasters. That is, many people imagine that, first, a disaster occurs; next, the world mobilizes to assist with emergency humanitarian aid; and then the disaster is over. **Everybody seems to think that when a disaster takes place, I hop the next plane to assist in the distribution of tents, blankets, medicine, and food. I don't do that.** A host of agencies and organizations, public and private, specializes in emergency assistance. Most of them could definitely use the assistance of a regionally knowledgeable anthropologist, but few emergency organizations, in fact, call on them.

However—and this is the part that is not generally appreciated—**a disaster is an unfolding process, beginning with socially constructed conditions of vulnerability in which a community lives.** The coincidence between a society and a natural or technological force brings about a socially configured set of conditions and processes we understand as a disaster. Emergency assistance is then mobilized, and relief operations begin. At some point when the situation is relatively stabilized, reconstruction plans are drawn up and another set of activities—themselves often configured by relief actions—are undertaken. **The reconstruction phase is the longest, most expensive, most complex and politically volatile of the disaster.** It potentially evokes the most profound changes in culture, society, and economy.

My work in disasters has focused almost entirely on the reconstruction phase. I have worked and/or researched in postearthquake reconstruction for ten years between 1970 and 1980 in Peru and, more recently, in post-hurricane reconstruction in Jamaica, the United States (briefly in post-Andrew Miami and post-Hugo South Carolina), and more recently in post-Mitch Honduras. Generally, **my focus has been on issues of postdisaster social organization, including class/race/ethnicity/gender differential patterns of aid distribution, social consensus and conflict, grief and mourning issues, and social mobilization of community-based reconstruction activities** such as housing and resettlement issues. I have also worked on post-hurricane housing education methods as a mitigation strategy. Most recently, my consultations for the World Bank in Honduras focused on the transition from relief to reconstruction with an emphasis on vulnerability reduction, employment generation, and resettlement issues.

There is currently a major multidisciplinary effort, in which I have been very involved, to direct attention toward the socially constructed conditions of vulnerability that prefigure a disaster and to reorient disaster assistance from a postdisaster replacement-driven reconstruction focus to a predisaster vulnerability reduction effort. **The goal today is to become proactive, linking vulnerability reduction to development, rather than continue to use a reactive and replacement orientation in reconstruction.** When a serious disaster has taken place, such as that in Honduras, the goals of reconstruction must be oriented to reduce future vulnerability, not merely to replace what was so vulnerable that it was destroyed.

Reference Cited

Oliver-Smith, Anthony
    1992[1986] The Martyred City: Death and Rebirth in the Andes. 2nd edition. Prospect
        Heights, IL: Waveland Press.

Originally appeared in Anthropology Newsletter, *November 1993*
Revised, spring 1998 and summer 1999